ParaConc and Parallel Corpora in Contrastive and Translation Studies

Michael Barlow

Athelstan
5925 Kirby Drive
Suite E 464
Houston TX 77005
info@athel.com

PREFACE

The first version of *ParaConc* was a rather rudimentary Macintosh program (based on Hypertalk) created in 1995. A few enthusiasts such as Pernilla Danielsson and Raf Salkie made some use of that program. In the following year work began on a Windows version, which led to the first beta version produced in 1996 and since that time numerous studies have been carried out using *ParaConc* within both the translation studies and contrastive analysis traditions.

This book is based on Build 269 of *ParaConc*. The version you are using may be slightly different---the version number is provided in ABOUT PARACONC in INFO menu.

CONTENTS

1. INTRODUCTION

Translating from one language to another is like trying to get into someone else's clothes. Sometimes the new clothes fit fairly well and at other times a considerable amount of retailoring is required in order to make the person look presentable in the new context. A translator must continually push here and squeeze there and add a stitch or two to successfully complete an acceptable transformation. When faced with the prospect of translating even simple phrases, the translator must try to match word choice, syntax, discourse, and register, along with the more subtle connotative aspects of meaning. There is no completely satisfactory translation—only the best compromise overall once the importance given to competing considerations is weighed.

Once this complex task is completed we have not only a translation, but a pair of equivalent texts in two languages and as analysts, rather than readers, we can start to think about repurposing these resulting texts to examine both the process of translation and the relationship between the two languages.

Analyses of the choices made by individual translators practising their art is naturally of interest in the field of translation studies (including translator training). One aspect of the form of translated texts that has been widely investigated in recent years is the fact that the translation process itself alters the structure of the language used due in part to the presence of the source language (Toury 1986). Features of translation include, according to Baker (1996), simplification, explicitation, and a tendency for the translated text to be influenced by the structures in the original text. This notion of 'translation universals,' while continuing to be controversial, has led to a considerable number of research studies: Laviosa (2002), Kenny (1999), among many others. Naturally, ParaConc can be used to investigate specific instances of translation features such as the presence of *that* complementizers.

Mauranen (2008) advocates a slightly different approach from Baker's. She suggests following the path of Greenberg's linguistic universals project in investigating tendencies rather than universal features and in distinguishing universals arising out of general cognitive processes from those derived from the functions of language in use.

The notion of translation as retailoring comes from the fact that different languages tend to be elaborated in different areas of grammar. English, for example, has a complex tense system, but very little grammatical coding of gender or social status. Consequently, part of the process of learning to be a translator involves the developing the skills and strategies to handle not only cultural issues, but in addition the differences in areas of elaboration.

ParaConc can be used to highlight the ways in different translators approach such difficulties. For instance, Wu and Chang (2008) examined translations of book *The Color Purple*, focussing on the treatment of the African-American Vernacular English used in dialogues in Alice Walker's book, The researchers searched for ***n't** in order to locate instances of *ain't* and double negative constructions such as *he don't say nothing*. They then examined how three different translators had approached the Chinese translation of these examples (Figure 1).

Figure 1: An English text and three Chinese translations

Linguists not working in translation studies tend to look at the picture that emerges from the accumulation of choices made by individual translators, the focus being the comparison and contrast of two (or more) languages rather than the translation process itself. What distinguishes the two approaches is a difference in granularity of the contrast. Translation studies research uses small texts where the influence of the translator is evident. The features of the translation footprint are likely to be apparent in the translation of a single book, for example. In contrast, the use of large corpora should help to "wash out" the influence of particular translations so that reliable equivalence data can be obtained for contrastive analysis.

Research based on the analysis of parallel corpora provide one good source of evidence regarding the nature of the translation process and the relationships holding between languages. Thus one aim here is to contribute to a new, corpus-based approach to translation studies and to contrastive analysis. The two approaches to parallel corpus analysis are mutually informing. The contrastive linguist learns about the nature of translated language, the third space; and the translation studies researcher learns about general relationships holding between two languages that can then inform the analysis of a particular text where something unusual may be in evidence.

It is impossible to make much progress on a contrastive analysis research program without confronting the issue of what counts as equivalence and what kind of equivalence we should be investigating. In the earlier era of Contrastive Analysis, Nickel (1971: 5) refers to the problem of equivalence, stating that while "formal equivalence can be established relatively easily", it is difficult to identify "functional-semantic equivalence". Identifying functional equivalence is unquestionably difficult, but identifying formal equivalence in a meaningful way is also not trivial. It is true that in one sense, establishing formal equivalence can be straightforward: establishing a link between the passive construction in French and the passive construction in English, for instance. At the time Nickel was writing, the equivalence between the two passives would be seen as a link between two language systems, i.e., two grammars.

Based on a Saussurean notion of language as a system and developed in terms of the phonological, morphological, syntactic systems of a language, the approach to contrastive analysis common in the 60s involved the creation of a contrastive grammar of two languages for some domain such as phonology or syntax (cf. Moulton 1962; Kufner 1962). Alternatively, following a notional approach, a particular word, construction, or semantic category is chosen and then the corresponding or "equivalent" items in two languages are investigated. For both approaches, the notion of "equivalence" and the problem of what to use as the basis of the comparison (*tertium comparationis*) is inescapable.

In what follows, we are using translation equivalence as the metric for comparison. Conceptually this is related to usage-based approaches to language, a term used for a variety of paradigms. The link here is the usage produced by the translator, who is not aiming to create equivalences, but rather to translate texts. Thus formal link between, say, passives in two languages is likely to be of no interest to most researchers if the two passive structures have little overlap in terms of usage. We are interested in form-meaning or form-function pairings, as discussed below. (See also Varadi and Kiss 2001).)

We can determine the extent of the usage overlap by calculating recurrent translation equivalence (Krzeszowski 1990: 27). In other words, examining the grammar of two languages and identifying a similar construction (e.g., passive) is only the first step. It is necessary to determine the correspondence in terms of usage of the formally equivalent structures. Unfortunately, usage or meaning or function cannot be identified automatically the way that forms can and it falls to the analyst to categorise the data according to their preferred theoretical constructs.

While the data available from translated texts is clearly of considerable interest, there remains the problem of how to approach the analysis of translations. *ParaConc* is a simple software program that makes it easy to analyse translated texts. It is designed primarily as a search tool designed to work with parallel texts. The program combined with a suitable set of texts can be used as a full context, bilingual dictionary or as linked bilingual discourses. There are differences, of course, in that the information is fairly raw, with all the advantages and disadvantages that rawness entails. The software is essentially a search engine, but it can be used to provide, on demand, a rich picture (in terms of co-text) of "translation equivalences" (with the caveats given above). Thus the software can present the user with (i) multiple instances of the search term and (ii) a large context for each instance of the search term, thereby allowing a thorough analysis of usage in terms of the equivalences between two languages.

We can use parallel corpora to search for congruence and non-congruence for particular language features, whether grammatical, such as reflexive constructions, or more lexical, such as prepositions (cf. Gellerstam 1996; Aijmer, Altenberg & Johansson 1996).

The absence of a wide range of parallel corpora is, without doubt, a major impediment, but as these difficulties are overcome, the full set of techniques and insights of corpus linguistics can be brought to bear on issues in contrastive and translation studies

The use of translated texts can be seen as a part of the wider notion of usage-based approaches to grammar. The term 'usage-based' was introduced in Langacker (1987) and explicated in more detail in Langacker (1988, 2000). A usage event is defined as a form-meaning pairing assembled by the speaker in a particular context for a particular purpose (Langacker 1987: 66). A usage-based approach, not surprisingly, assumes that the primary object of study is the language people actually produce and understand, rather than an abstraction based on intuitions about grammaticality. Furthermore, a working assumption is that language in use provides good evidence of the nature and organization of linguistic systems. On this view, there is an intimate relation between grammatical structures and instances of use. The connection between usage and grammar is not straightforward, but again the assumption is that grammar gives rise to usage and usage gives rise to grammar (Kemmer & Barlow 2000).

The analysis of corpora provides information on usage and hence can lead to insights into the nature of grammar. The usage-based approach can be extended to cover translation by viewing usage in terms of connections between form-meaning pairs in two languages. Again, this is not a simple relationship since knowing two languages does not necessarily mean that it is a straightforward task to translate from one to the other. There exists a process of learning to translate which precedes any actual translation. In other words, the translator must acquire knowledge of links between forms in both languages, mediated by appropriate meanings and other expertise that enables translation.

The success of monolingual corpus analyses in providing particular insights into the form and functioning of language in use provides a foundation for studies of parallel corpora. The first and most obvious contribution is in highlighting the pervasiveness and the range of functions of collocations (Pawley and Syder 1983; Sinclair 1991; Kelljmer 1994) and other syntagmatic units with a lexical component. These units come in a variety of shapes and sizes, and are referred by a variety of names: chunks, prefabricated units, lexical bundles, etc. Although they are notoriously difficult to classify, this level of linguistic structure, somewhere between individual words and more abstract syntactic structures, carries a high functional load in languages. Not surprisingly, this type of lexicogrammatical unit has also been proposed as a minimal unit of translation.

The second major contribution of corpus linguistics is in highlighting and quantifying variability in language. The extent of variability has been masked to some degree by the use of intuition data in theoretical linguistics, and, indeed, one of the very motivations for using intuition data in the first place is to abstract away from patterns of variation. Corpus studies have, however, brought new aspects of variation into perspective, including considerable work on register and text types (Biber 1988), local grammars (Hunston and Sinclair 2000), and variation in lexicogrammatical expressions. The translation process adds a further dimension to the potential for variation.

The third major influence of corpus studies relates to the provision of frequency information, and with that tends to come an emphasis on typical forms of expression rather than on the range of possible forms of expression. The consequence for contrastive studies is that we can establish three sets of relations. The first is general equivalence, in other words we can ask the question, for an expression in Language A, what range of expressions might be equivalent in Language B? To establish this general map of equivalence, we are taking account of translation equivalences that occur at least once. And it is in this regard that there are limitations in the use of corpora for two reasons. One is the simple fact that corpora are samples, which means that some equivalences will not occur in any particular sample – and this will be particularly true for word combinations. The second limitation is that some equivalences may be more the result or byproduct of the translation process rather a true equivalence in the two languages. However, if in this case we find that an equivalence occurs when translating from Language A to Language B, and also when going from Language B to Language A, then we can feel confident that the particular relationship between the two languages is real.

Using corpus analysis tools it is possible to go beyond general equivalence and give a quantitative view of equivalence, which from a usage perspective is potentially more important. For a word or collocation or construction in language A we can ask what the most common translation equivalents are, and similarly for language B. Using frequency data it is possible to build up a more detailed equivalence map and describe the central translation equivalents. This frequency equivalence is complex in a couple of ways. First of all, if we look at the frequency distribution of a word in a single language, we typically find that the core or prototypical usage is not the most frequent. Thus for *see*, the 'seeing with the eyes' meaning is not the most frequent in texts. We can, of course, still uncover instances where the prototype use in Language A is equivalent to the prototype use in Language B. Thus for the verb *go*, we find the examples in (1) in which *go* has the prototypical meaning of movement from one physical location to another. The equivalent sentence in French uses the equivalent verb *aller*.

(1)   Mr. Donelly often goes to the United States.

             M. Donelly va souvent aux États-Unis.

Looking at a sample of the data, we discover that only around 10% of the instances of *go*, including *go* plus particle, could be considered prototypical (in the sense of used in the basic domain of motion through space), with the majority of uses, including various collocations and phrasal verbs, being associated with a more extended metaphorical meaning, where the movement associated with *go* is located within a conceptual rather than physical space. Some examples are *go a long way to, go ahead, go along with, go beyond, go hand in hand, go in for*, and *go through*. Hence we observe the skewed frequency pattern for a particular expression where the prototypical or basic meaning is rather infrequent in most texts; some extended meanings are highly frequent; while yet other non-prototypical meanings are infrequent. Next we need a third frequency calculation for the equivalence relation itself, since any particular expression in Language A will have a probabilistic relationship with a set of expressions in Language B, taking a 1: 1 relationship to be at the limit of the probabilistic range.

Of particular interest here is the congruence in particular forms in two languages. For example, we can use the software to examine the congruence between the English verb *go* and the French verb *aller*. How likely is *go* to be translated by *aller* and how likely is *aller* to be translated by *go*? This may be an appropriate question at this most coarse level of granularity for some equivalences, but for highly polysemous expressions such as *go*, a more fine-grained investigation is usually needed in order to consider the different senses or uses of *go* and the extent each sense/use is likely to correspond to an equivalent expression based on *aller*. The advantage of the usage-based approach advocated here is that we do not simply rely on intuitions to judge congruence. We can obtain quantitative information on correspondences between two languages, which gives us a somewhat more objective picture of the degree of correspondence of patterns. There are, as we might expect, some caveats associated with the use of correspond-ence data, in addition to those mentioned above. For one thing the frequency data will vary to some extent depending on the type of corpus used in the analysis. Another problem is that if the numbers are very large, it is not feasible to check every *go-aller* pair to ensure that the two words are in fact equivalent and not simply by chance co-occurring in their respective text segments. To mitigate this problem, we can check a sample and make any necessary adjustments to the frequency data if we find chance cooccurrence. Third, it must be said that corpus data typically needs to be interpreted, and so intuitions about language are not eliminated completely. Rather, the idea is that the interpretation is carried out on the more solid basis of quantitative empirical data.

2. ParaConc: A Multilingual Concordance Program

We can begin with a brief practical introduction to parallel concordancing using ParaConc before examining the wider perspective of the use of parallel corpora in contrastive and translation studies. Our aim is to explore the use of parallel corpora (translation corpora) to highlight the nature of translation or the styles of particular translators, or more broadly to investigate patterns across different languages, but before doing that, let us deal with some practical details.

QUICK LOOK

To start the program, double-click on the file ParaConc. Once the software opens, a simple screen appears, as shown below in Figure 2. This initial screen looks rather bare, containing only a blank window and two menu items: FILE and INFO.

Figure 2: Initial screen

Note that the information field in the lower left corner states: "No files loaded."

1ˢᵗ search

Since we are dealing with multiple languages and multiple windows, some complexity is unavoidable, but it is nevertheless possible to load and search corpus files quickly and easily. To illustrate this and to get an overview of the operation of *ParaConc*, you can follow the instructions below to carry out a simple text search. If you would rather follow a more methodical, step-by-step introduction, then you should skip to the next part of this section on page 19. If you need some aligned parallel files, you can download some European Parliament data from http://www.statmt.org/europarl/.

1. Choose LOAD CORPUS FILE(S) from the FILE menu. Set the number of parallel texts to 2.

2. Select the language of each set of texts by clicking on the language textbox.

3. Select one or more text files for each language using the add (and remove?) buttons. If you run into problems later, it may be because the files were out of order or there was some other problem related to alignment.

4. Click on open. When the files are being loaded, progress bars will appear as each file is processed.

5. Choose search from the search menu.

6. Choose a language to work with and enter a search string (a word or phrase). Click OK (or press return).

7. Press return (or click Cancel) if you wish to halt the search at any time.

8. Examine the results in the concordance window. The hits will be easier to view if you maximise the window. Click on a line that is of interest and you will see that the corresponding line or segment in the second half of the window will be highlighted.

9. Try sorting the concordance lines, using commands in the SORT menu to look for different patterns in the data.

10. Try different display options by using CONTEXT TYPE and SHOW LINE NUMBERS. Delete any unwanted examples by selecting the lines and pressing Ctrl-D or by selecting DELETE from the DISPLAY menu.

11. Possible translations (in the lower text window) can be identified (or highlighted) in a couple of ways. You can position the cursor in the lower window, click on the right

mouse button, and select SEARCH QUERY from the pop-up menu. Enter the possible translation and press return. Choose CONTEXT TYPE from the DISPLAY menu and choose WORDS. You will then get a KWIC format in the lower window, which can be sorted via the SORT menu. Thus the display/sort menus control whichever text is selected. This is important: the menu commands are sensitive to whichever text or language is currently selected.

no hits? If, contrary to your expectations, the search returned no finds or "hits," then it is likely to be either due to a problem with the specification of the search string because the word or phrase you looked for is not present in the text.

FILE and INFO Having given a brief overview, let us return to the beginning and work more methodically through the different aspects of the program.

2.1 Selecting a corpus

Let us examine the options for loading a corpus, that is, making one or more text files available for processing by *ParaConc*. This operation is initiated by choosing LOAD CORPUS FILE(S) from the FILE menu (Figure 3) or by issuing the CTRL-L command.

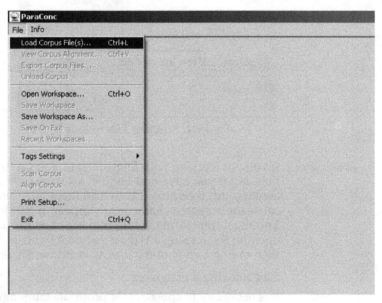

Figure 3: File menu

When the LOAD CORPUS FILE(S) command is given, a dialogue box as shown in Figure 4 appears, enabling particular parallel files to be loaded. The heading PARALLEL

19

TEXTS at the top of the dialogue box is followed by a number in the range 2-4. We will assume for now that we are dealing with texts in two languages and will choose 2—although the procedure is essentially the same if you are dealing with four languages, or an original text and three translations.

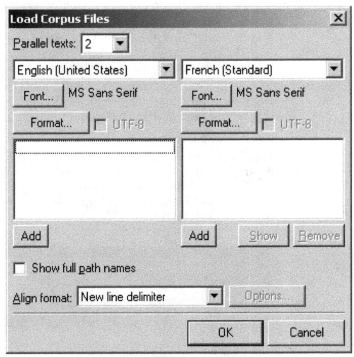

Figure 4: Selecting files making up the corpus

gárblèd accents If you are working with English texts, you can use ASCII files, but if you have non-English ASCII files containing accents, etc., then attempts to load them into *ParaConc* will cause the accented characters to appear in garbled form. You must transform the files into ANSI text format by opening them using a Windows-based word-processor and then saving a copy of the files as Windows (ANSI) text.

2.2 Choosing a Language

Luo/Thai It is necessary to choose an appropriate language for each set of texts. The available languages can be seen by clicking on the drop-down arrow to the right of the language name. Apart from providing a label for each set of texts, choosing a language allows special character and accents to be entered easily, and defines the appropriate alphabetical (sorting) order. (The range of languages displayed will depend on the version and configuration of Windows installed on your machine.) If the language you want is not present in the list, you should simply select the font that you want to use.

2.3 Adding Files

When the ADD button is selected, the typical Windows dialogue box appears in which the contents of the current directory are displayed. Alternative directories/drives can be selected via the text box at the top of the dialogue box

Once the appropriate file name appears, use the mouse to click on the filename to select it. To select several files, use the shift and cursor keys, or CTRL-A (or to select non-adjacent files, use Ctrl and shift and click). The result should be similar to the example in Figure 5.

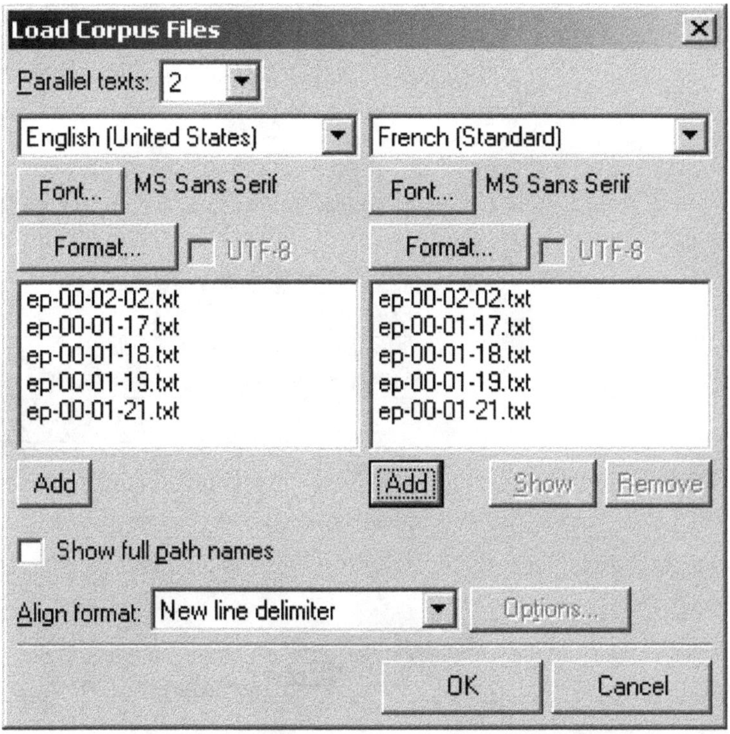

Figure 5: Adding English and French files

reorder files   The files for each language should be listed in appropriate (parallel) order. This is crucial. If they are out of order, it is possible to "click and drag" them so that they are in their proper place.

| alignment | The text segments in these files are already aligned and so all that is needed is to select the appropriate alignment indicator. The text segments in these files are delimited by means of a carriage return (paragraph mark) and so we choose the NEW LINE DELIMITED SEGMENTS setting for ALIGN FORMAT. Symbols other than a carriage return may be used and in this case the appropriate option is DELIMITED SEGMENTS. To indicate the alignment symbol used, click on options and enter the symbol in the text box. |

| multiple files | Further control over the display of file names is accomplished by entering a combination of characters and * in the box FILE NAME in the lower part of the dialogue box. Here it is possible to enter a string such as **g*.spo** (and press the return key) in order to display just those files that start with a G and have the extension SPO. Once the appropriate file name appears, use the mouse to click on the filename to select it. To select several files, use the shift and cursor keys, or CTRL-A (or to select non-adjacent files, use Ctrl and shift and click). |

| odd results | If you find that after carrying out a search that the lower window contains a single sentence repeated over and over, then it is likely to be a problem arising out of the incorrect setting of the alignment scheme or alignment delimiter. |

The different alignment options are shown in Figure 6.

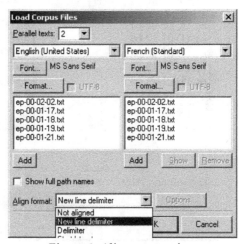

Figure 6: Alignment options

An alternative scheme available in the current version is based on the use of start/stop tags. Thus aligned segments may be indicated by the segment start and end tags <seg> and </seg>. Alternatively, a COCOA format may be used in which the start tag contains alignment information internally in the form of an attribute, as in <seg ID=245>. The particulars of this type of configuration can be specified once the SEGMENT START/STOP MARKERS alignment option is selected.

unicode

The current version of *ParaConc* can deal with 2 byte characters, but not with unicode. If the text files are in unicode, they must be selected and the unicode checkbox must be selected. This will translate the files into ANSI format for formatting by *ParaConc*.

2.4 Loading the corpus

Clicking on OPEN (or pressing Return) loads the selected files into *ParaConc*, making them available for searching. As discussed below, the program scans through the pairs of files looking for information about tags and alignment. When the scanning process is completed, the word count for the two corpora will appear at the lower right of the window. The processing of the files may take some time and it is advisable to use the workspace option (described in Chapter 7) to minimise the number of times that this operation has to be performed.

corpus size

There is no real limit to the size of the corpus loaded. The corpus files appear to be loaded in the program ready for searching, but in reality *ParaConc* does not load the whole text, but switches chunks of text in and out of memory as needed, which means that the program should theoretically be able to handle any size of text. There will be some limits depending on the particular configuration of the computer being used.

Once a corpus is loaded, some new menu items related to the analysis and display of the text appear on the menu bar. These are FILE, SEARCH, FREQUENCY, and INFO. In addition, looking at the screen in Figure 7 we see information in the lower left corner relating to the number of the files loaded and in the lower right corner a word count for the two corpora. The corpus itself is not displayed, although it can be viewed if necessary, as described below.

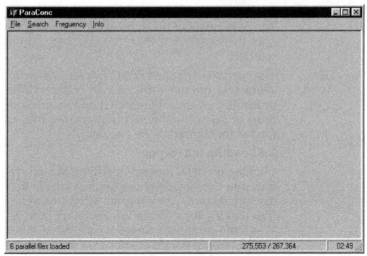

Figure 7: View of ParaConc after files have been loaded

Before initiating a text search, we should note that despite the fact that we have one or more files loaded and a window showing the text of the first of these files, the choices made so far can be changed very easily

2.5 Displaying the corpus files

corpus view   The loaded corpora are not displayed on screen, but any of the corpus files can be viewed if desired. The main method viewing files is to select the command VIEW CORPUS FILE(S) (Ctrl-V) from the FILE menu. A dialogue box containing the file system is displayed. This option allows you to examine parallel files. If the ALIGNMENT button is clicked, then the alignment menu becomes available, as described above. If the SHOW button is selected, then the parallel files are displayed side by side and a new menu CORPUS TEXT appears. The commands in CORPUS TEXT are CHANGE FONT, SUPPRESS, WORD WRAP, EQUAL WIDTHS and SYNCHRONIZE TEXTS. The first three commands control the display of the text. The vertical bar separating the files can be adjusted to allow more space for the display of one of the languages and the EQUAL WIDTHS command simply readjusts the display to give equal horizontal space to each language. If SYNCHRONIZE TEXTS is selected, scrolling through one file will cause the parallel files to scroll.

2.6 Changing the corpus

unload corpus   In addition to manipulating the form of the corpus files, it is possible to alter the actual composition of the corpus. For instance, all the files may be removed by choosing UNLOAD CORPUS from the FILE menu. This returns the program to its initial state, with only the FILE and INFO menus available. All other windows and menus are closed.

remove files The selective removal of one or more files is accomplished by selecting LOAD CORPUS FILE(S) from the FILE menu, selecting one or more files and clicking on the REMOVE button. Additional files can be added by selecting LOAD CORPUS FILE(S) and clicking the ADD button.

2.7 Maintaining different subcorpora

One good way of organising and accessing different corpora is to maintain each subcorpus as a workspace. This option will use up a certain amount of disk space, but the advantage is that clicking on a single (appropriately named) file will load a sub-corpus, along with the settings for that sub-corpus. For more information on workspaces, see Chapter 7.

2.8 Printing the corpus files

Setting up the printer is accomplished by the command PRINT SETUP in the FILE menu. (To specify the default printer, use the control panel.) If you want to print the current corpus file, the one in the active window, select PRINT from the CORPUS TEXT menu or enter CTRL-P. Since the corpus file may be large and the print command may be selected in error, a dialogue box appears, giving an estimate of the size of the file. The print job can then be cancelled if necessary.

3. Searching for metaphors

Any phrase involving the word "metaphor" inevitably opens up a number of domains and endless interpretative possibilities. Academics in the different language-related disciplines generally spend a considerable amount of time searching, consciously or unconsciously, for metaphors that adequately capture their perspective on issues related to language analysis. Here I will be more prosaic and simply consider the issue of how to search for metaphors. A concordance program can be seen both as very sophisticated and as very simple. A monolingual concordancer such as *ParaConc's* sister program *MonoConc* is basically a search program that looks for patterns in the text based on a search query. Simple as this sounds, it can lead to sophisticated analyses of lexical, grammatical and textual structure by allowing the researcher to easily find rare instances of words or strings; find strings in the context of other strings, e.g., the instances of *economy* occurring after <title> and before </title>; and trawl through large texts looking for particular patterns. The results can then be rearranged and concentrated so that the properties of the search item can be revealed.

We can also view a concordancer as very basic in the sense that we cannot enter a search for metaphors or *wh*-clefts or downtoners or apologies. We typically search for words or meta information in the form of tags that have been added to the corpus. Searching for metaphors, then, means searching for words contained in the metaphors and so for body part metaphors, we search for *head, foot, back* etc.

Of course, here we are looking at a multilingual concordancer, which adds an important new dimension to the search process. Let us illustrate this with a simple search for the English word *head* in an English-French parallel corpus. To initiate the search, we select SEARCH from the SEARCH menu, or enter CTRL-S, (shown in Figure 8).

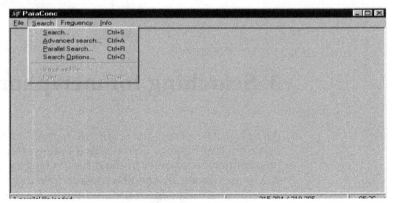

Figure 8: Search menu

simple search   In the text box at the top of the dialogue box that appears (Figure 9) type in the search term **head** and click on OK (or press enter). The example search queries that can be found below the search box serve to remind us about the format of simple text searches—and the use of wildcards. Notice too that a search can be performed on either language. This is controlled by the choice under LANGUAGE at the top of the dialogue box.

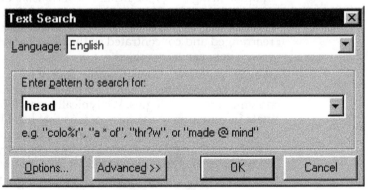

Figure 9: Performing a simple text search

Note: The parameters of the search are determined by the settings in force in GENERAL SEARCH CONTROL in the ADVANCED SEARCH dialogue box and in SEARCH OPTIONS as illustrated in Figure 10. These latter settings cover such things as whether the hyphen is treated a word boundary. (See Chapter 10 for a complete description.)

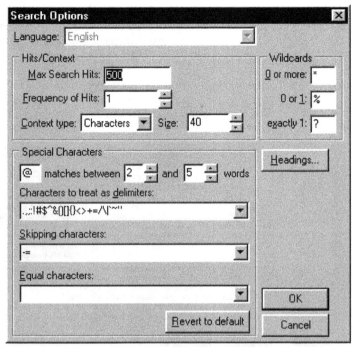

Figure 10: Settings in Search Options

Once the search query has been entered, the program starts to work though the loaded files looking for the search string. If a search does not behave in the way that you expect, then this is probably because (a) the corpus is not quite what you thought it was; (b) the search term was mistyped; or (c) some setting (such as the list of word delimiters) is not what you expected.

Let us now look in some detail at what happens during the search process. In our example, the program works through the text looking for the word *head*. With such a common word, the results should come in at a fairly rapid clip. Two progress bars track the progression of the search routine as it scans (i) individual files and (ii) the corpus as a whole.

stop search

To stop a search, but retain the hits already found, simply press return or click Cancel. (If pressing return has no effect, simply click on the progress box to make it active.)

The progress bars remain visible as long as the search is still in progress. The results of the search appear in a backgrounded window, which we will refer to as the concordance results window (Figure 11). This window might seem a little daunting at first due to the arrangement of blocks of text which differ markedly from the normal text layout found in books and documents. Note that the text

29

results in this example are divided into two parts
(separated by an adjustable bar). In the top part of the
window, each instance of the search word that the program
finds is copied along with a preceding and following
context. Typically, the search word is centred and
highlighted so that the instances of the search word line up,
as shown in Figure 11. This format is commonly referred to
as a KWIC (Key Word In Context) format.

KWIC

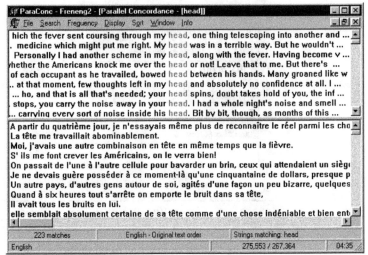

Figure 11: Concordance results in a KWIC format

Words surrounding the keyword may also be highlighted.
This highlighting indicates potential collocates of the
searchword. See Section 5.4 for a discussion of this feature.

3.1 Results in Two Languages

English/French The lower part of the window contains the French
sentences (or, more strictly, text segments) that are aligned
with the hits displayed in the top window. This process is
not at all magical; it is a consequence of the alignment
process. Thus if the first instance of *head* occurred in
segment 342 of the English text, then the program simply
displays segment 342 of the French text in the lower
window, with this process being repeated for all instances
of *head*. It is worth thinking about this for a moment in
order to fully understand how the parallel concordancer
works and how important it is to interpret the results with
caution. Thus we are working with (assumed) equivalence
at the sentence or segment level, and within this
equivalence, we can use the program to help determine
word or phrase equivalents, but there is no guarantee that

an English word highlighted in the KWIC display will be translated in the equivalent French sentence. The program is simply indicating the sentence or text segment that is equivalent on the basis of alignment to the English sentence that contains the keyword.

3.2 Sorting and categorising the results

sort

Let's follow this example further. One typical way of carrying out a contrastive study is to analyse and categorise the instances in one language. This allows the categorisation and grouping (i.e., sorting) of concordance lines according to user-defined categories. Thus if you have five categories or classifications that are appropriate for a set of concordance results, you can assign the letter *a, b, c, d,* or *e*, as appropriate, to each line. To do this, select (click on) a concordance line, click on the right mouse button and assign a letter to that line. (See Figure 12.)

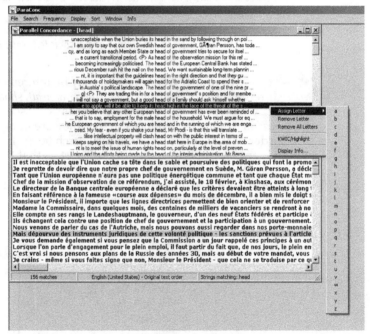

Figure 12: Assigning letters in order to categorise the results

The assigned letter is then displayed to the left of each concordance line (Figure 13) and the results can be sorted (using ADVANCED SORT) according to your assigned categories.

Figure 13: Letter categories are associated with each line

To take a simpler example, you may be interested in different uses of *head*: *big head, company head, shower head,* etc. One way to find out which words are associated with *head* is to sort the instances so that they are in alphabetical order of the word preceding the search term. The advantage of performing this 'left sort' is that the modifiers (adjectives) of *head* that are the same will occur together. The easiest way to achieve this ordering is to select 1ST LEFT, 1ST RIGHT, from the SORT menu (Figure 14).

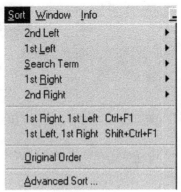

Figure 14: The Sort menu

The program then immediately rearranges the concordance lines in a way that typically groups the results in revealing ways. If you are interested in one particular example of *head* in English, we can click on the appropriate line and both the English and French lines will be highlighted, as shown in Figure 15. (Notice also the sorted lines in the upper text window.)

You can glance at the words directly preceding *head* to check that the intended re-ordering has taken place. Alternatively, you can check the description of the current sort that appears at the bottom of the results window, to the right of the information on the number of hits. Having ordered the concordance lines in this way, it is very easy to see which words occur with *head* and with what frequency. In *ParaConc*, specifying a sorting order typically involves selecting a primary sort position (e.g., 1st Left) and a secondary sort position (e.g., 1st Right). See Chapter 9 for a detailed explanation of sorting.

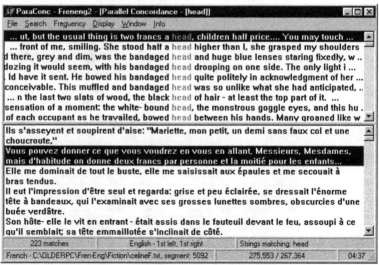

Figure 15: Sorted concordance results

If you scroll fairly quickly through the concordance results, you will discover that the visual patterning created by several identical words surrounding the search word will be striking enough to catch your eye. It is not necessary to focus on the results line by line; you can scan the output quite rapidly. You can also click examples of interest and examine the corresponding sentence in the French text. Conversely, it is also possible to click on a French sentence and examine the English sentence. Notice that as you alternately click on the lower and upper windows, both the language indicator and the filename in the lower left of the screen change. Thus it is possible to make either the English text active or the French text active. This is important since, as we will see, we will want to use the menu items to manipulate the French results as well as the English results.

3.3 Suggesting Translations

It can be difficult to locate the position of possible French translations of *head* within each French segment. To alleviate this, we can highlight suggested translations for English *head* by positioning the cursor in the lower French results window and clicking on the right mouse button. The menu shown in Figure 16 pops up and the user can select SEARCH QUERY which gives access to the usual search commands. You can enter a possible translation such as *tête*.

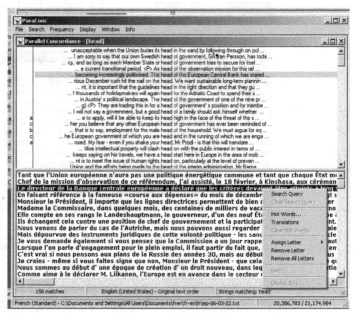

Figure 16: Pop-up menu

The program then simply highlights all instances of *tête* in the French results window, as illustrated in Figure 17. (The translations are normally in red, which will not show up well here.)

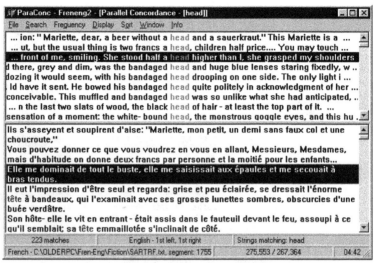

Figure 17: Highlighting possible translations

3.4 KWIC Results II

KWIC II

We can now change the context for the French results so that the results in the lower window are transformed into a KWIC layout (at least for those segments containing *tête.)* First, we make sure that the lower window is active. (Look at the lower left of the window to check that a French file is selected or simply click within the French text window.) Next we choose CONTEXT TYPE from the DISPLAY menu and select WORDS. Finally, we rearrange the lines to bring those segments containing *tête* together at the top of the French results window. To achieve this, choose SORT and sort the lines by search word, and 1st left. The sorting procedure will now rearrange the results in lower window since the sort commands are applied to whichever window is active. The two text windows then appear as shown in Figure 20. This sequence can be accomplished using a shortcut. Simply click on the right mouse button when the cursor is within the French results window and select KWIC from the menu.

Naturally, only those words in the French text that have been selected and highlighted can be displayed in this way. By sorting on the searchword, all the KWIC lines are grouped together at the top of the text window; the residue, which may be quite large, can be found by scrolling through towards the bottom of the window.

This is a revealing display, but we have to avoid being misled by the dual KWIC displays. There is no guarantee that for any particular line, the instance of *tête* is the

35

translation of *head*. It could be accidental that *tête* is found in the French segment that corresponds to the English segment containing *head*.

The idea behind this feature of *ParaConc* is to let the user move from English to French and back again, massaging the results to get a sense of the connections between the two languages.

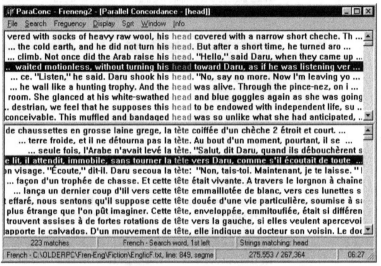

Figure 18: Two KWIC Displays

Let me remind you once more that the display and sort menus are sensitive to which of the windows is active. The information panels at the bottom of the screen will provide information on the current state of the program.

3.5 Hot Words

In the previous section, we used SEARCH QUERY to locate possible translations in the second window. In this section we will look at a utility in which possible translations and other associated words (collocates) are suggested by the program itself. We will call these words: hotwords. (These are sometimes called keywords.) First we position the cursor in the lower (French) half of the results window and click using the right mouse button. If we used SEARCH QUERY earlier, we need to select CLEAR SEARCH QUERY and then we can choose HOT WORDS, which brings up a dialogue box containing a ranked list of hot words. The ranked list of candidates for hotwords are displayed as shown in Figure 19. The figures can be taken as an approximate guide to the relative strength of the different words.

Figure 19: Hot Word List

Some or all the words can be selected. When the list of selected words is complete, click on OK. The words will be highlighted in the results and can again be sorted. A new sorted list is shown in Figure 20.

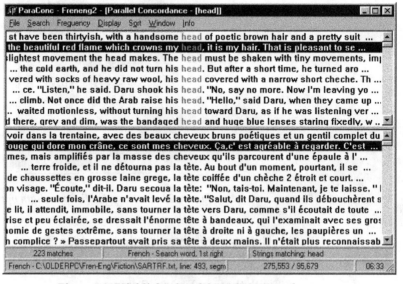

Figure 20: Highlighted and Sorted Hot Words

3.6 Translation Option

It is also possible to change the algorithm in order to attempt to isolate translations rather than hot words. Again we position the cursor in the lower half of the results window and click using the right mouse button. Select the translation option and set the number of candidate translations required. The algorithm for translation is very similar to that of hotwords, but it aims to eliminate the collocates. How well this works depends on factors such as the number of hits and the morphological complexity of the language involved.

3.7 Paradigm Option

One problem using calculations based on word comparison to provide a list of hotwords arises from the fact that words which are very similar, such as *tête* and *têtes,* are treated as completely different words. We need some way to boost the ranking of words whose forms are similar. To do this we select OPTIONS in Hotwords and check Paradigm option, as shown in Figure 21.

Figure 21: Settings for the paradigm option

The results of choosing the paradigm option should compensate, to some extent, for the lack of a morphological analysis of words. The results in Figure 22 can be compared with those in Figure 19 above.

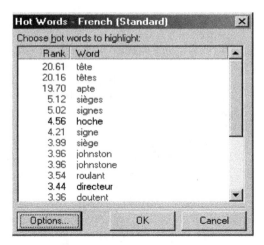

Figure 22: Results with paradigm option selected

3.8 Context Window

We have seen that the results of a search are displayed in KWIC format in the concordance results window. To see a larger context (i.e., a chunk of preceding and following text) for any concordance line, simply select the line in the results window by double-clicking on it. This larger context is then displayed in a new context window.

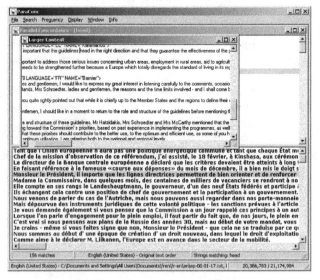

Figure 23: Context window

3.9 Using Wildcards

Let us consider again our search for *head*. To broaden the search, we can make use of wildcard characters. (We will discuss more precise and sophisticated alternatives in Section 4.1.)

* wildcard

The first wildcard character is the asterisk *. This wildcard in a search string will match zero or more characters and so we can use it to formulate a more complex search string with a wider range of potential matches than would be possible using a fully specified search string. Thus a search for **head*** will find *head, heads, header, heading*, etc.

delete results

Searching for the **head*** string produces numerous hits. Since we are not sure what words are found by this search, we need to sort the concordance lines with respect to the search word. This means that the lines are sorted according to the alpha-betical order of all the words that fit the template **head***. To accomplish this, choose SEARCH TERM, 1ST RIGHT from the SORT menu. Once we have done this, we can scroll through the concordance window, checking the search word. We may notice words that are not of interest and we can press CTRL-D to delete those particular lines (or select DELETE ITEM from the DISPLAY menu). (Eventually, it will be possible to select (and delete) multiple lines.

? wildcard

The wildcard character ? stands for a single alphanumeric character. In the unlikely event that we wanted to search for *head* or *heed*, we could find both words by searching for **he?d**.

% wildcard

The special character % represents zero or one character. Thus the search string **head%** would match *head* and *heads*.

* alone

It is a feature of *ParaConc* that it does not require there to be an alphanumeric character within the search string. You might like to think about the results of a search for * by itself.

If you want to search for question mark (?) as a literal character, you will have to substitute a different character for the wildcard in the SEARCH OPTIONS dialogue box. (See Section 10.8)

Below is a summary of the wildcard characters relevant for a TEXT SEARCH:

*	matches zero or more alphanumeric characters
%	matches zero or one character
?	matches exactly one character

3.10 Saving the Concordance Lines

To save the contents of the concordance window, select SAVE AS FILE from the CONCORDANCE menu. A dialogue box appears and the name of the results file can be entered.

show names   The default option is to save just the concordance results in the file. However, there are a variety of options concerning other information that can be saved along with the concordance lines. Checking the box FILE NAMES ON EACH LINE causes a preceding filename to be saved with each concordance line. The filename indicates the file in the corpus that the concordance line is associated with. Other options are SEQUENTIAL NUMBER IN EACH LINE, CONCEAL HITS, LINE NUMBERS, SEGMENTS, PAGE NUMBER, and NORMAL TAGS. (If PAGE NUMBER is selected, then RELATIVE LINES may be selected if you want to see the line number of the hit relative to the page rather than the line number in the file as a whole.) The SUPPRESS option allows you to suppress words or tags. To save the concordance lines, enter a suitably descriptive file name and press the enter key (or click on OK).

For further manipulation of the text, you may need to load the results file into a word processing program such as *Word*.

If only a few examples are needed, it may be more convenient to use CTRL-C to copy the required text directly from within *ParaConc* to the clipboard and then paste it into your document.

3.11 Printing the Concordance Results

The concordance lines can be printed by entering CTRL-P or selecting PRINT from the CONCORDANCE menu. The appropriate concordance window must be active for printing to occur.

4. The Search For Syntax

Summary: Select ADVANCED SEARCH from the
CONCORDANCE menu, choose TEXT SEARCH, REGULAR
EXPRESSION, or TAG SEARCH and enter the search string
appropriate for the type of search selected. The
parameters controlling the search are listed in SEARCH
OPTIONS. The ADVANCED SEARCH command contains other
refinements: APPEND SEARCH, and HEADINGS/CONTEXT
search.

Many linguists working on syntax are considering how
corpus resources can be used to provide data for linguistic
analyses. A discussion of the role of corpora in syntactic
analyses is well beyond the scope of this book, but we can
distinguish two ways to approach corpus data: corpus-
based and corpus-driven analyses (Tognini-Bonelli 2001).
Corpus-based and corpus-driven analyses differ in the
importance for the analysis of the empirical data in a
corpus. The underpinnings of a corpus-based approach
might come from a theory or conjecture and the corpus is
seen as providing some examples to support or reject a
theoretical position. The assumption in a corpus-drive
approach is that the analyses has to account for or reflect
the data found in a corpus

Finding syntactic patterns in untagged text necessarily
means searching for words and making use of punctuation
wherever possible. In section 3.9 in the previous chapter,
we saw ways of searching the passive using a simple text
search and wild card characters and here we will explore
the more powerful regular expression search.

Unfortunately, there is no magic way to extract syntactic
patterns. We can only follow the sorts of mundane
formulations of search strings that one might come up with.
And it has to be said that there is a certain amount of trial
and error in formulating a search string that gets the best
results, and, as always, there will be a tension between
precision and recall. Selecting the SENTENCE MODE checkbox
in ADVANCED SEARCH may improve precision since this will
not allow search string to cross a sentence boundary, which
may happen if the search involves several words. Of course,
if you use sentence mode, then you cannot use a search
string such as *. There to find sentence-initial *there*. And

perhaps a case-sensitive search for **There** will yield the same results in this case—and it would also find sentence-initial *there* that followed a sentence ending in a question mark.

4.1 Regular Expression Search

We will be able to perform reasonable searches using the simple search option, but if we are working with non-tagged texts, it is best to explore the use of regular expressions since they provide a level of control that will allow you to formulate complex, precise searches.

The full complexity of regular expressions, a well-defined set of string operators, can be overwhelming at first, but it is certainly possible to make immediate use of the simpler aspects of regular expressions and to build up complex searches step-by-step. It is useful to refer to previous regular expression searches saved in the search history list, and if you create a particularly useful regular expression, you might want to use the load/save feature of BATCH SEARCH to store the search query in a file so that search strings can be retrieved rather than re-created.

Some searches lend themselves to the use of regular expressions. An example is a search for a variety of body metaphors: *head, foot, eye, hand,* etc. Searching for syntactic patterns such as the passive by making use of lexical or morphological regularities is another common use. We will use as an example the search for a lemma or word family.

AND, OR, NOT

To initiate a regular expression (regex) search, select the radio button labelled REGULAR EXPRESSION located on the left side of the ADVANCED SEARCH dialogue box. See Figure 21. Note that three examples of regular expression searches appear under the search text box, as an aid to remembering the appropriate form of regex search queries.

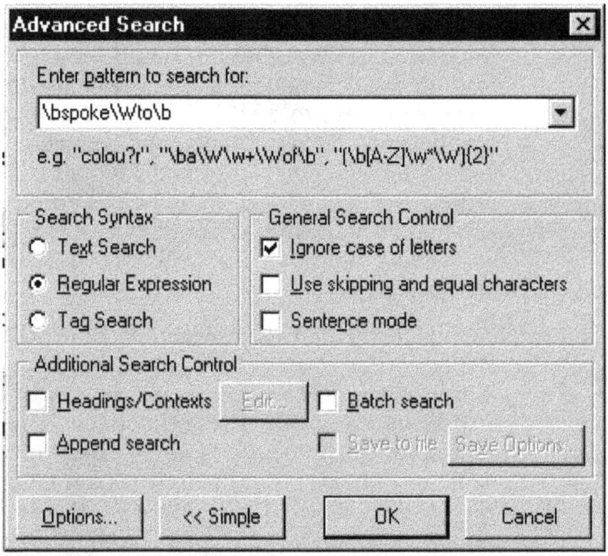

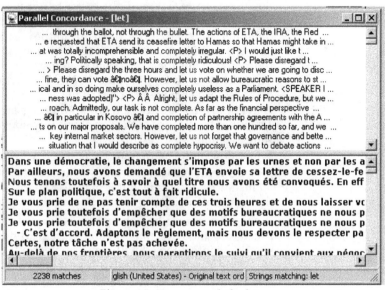

Figure 24: A search using a regular expression

string search   Regex searches are string searches, which means that the
computer searches for the string anywhere in the text,
regardless of word boundaries or other surrounding text.
Thus, if *let* is specified as the search term, then *bullet, letter,*
and *completely* are all potential matches for this search term.
See Figure 25.

Figure 25: Regex search for let

\<word\>	Because regex searches are string searches, word boundaries must be indicated explicitly and there are a variety of ways to do this. The basic method is to use symbols for the left and right boundaries, \< and \>, as in **\<let\>**. Or, if you wish to find words starting with the letter z, you could search for **\<z**. If you try this, you will see that only the initial z of the word is highlighted and to order the z words in alphabetical order you must choose a 1st right sort.
	Similarly, if you wish to find words ending in z, you can search for **z\>**.
\bword\b	A more general and slightly easier way of specifying a word boundary is by using the meta-character **\b**. Thus a search for *let* can be specified as **\blet\b**. Meta-characters such as \b typically come in complementary pairs and in this case the alternative symbol is \B, which stands for a non-word boundary. Thus a search for **\Bz\B** will find all those words which contain z surrounded by non-word boundaries—that is, by other letters or numbers.
delimiter\W	How can a search for the phrase *spoke to* be specified? One way to capture this is by means of the search string **\bspoke\b \bto\b**, which includes the space character between the two word boundary symbols. One alternative to entering the space character is to use the whitespace meta-character **\s**, which covers both space and tab. However, whitespace does not cover all word delimiters and therefore in order to avoid missing some instances of the phrase *spoke to* it might be better to use the meta-character **\W**, which stands for any symbol that is a word delimiter; in other words, it covers all the characters listed as word delimiters in SEARCH OPTIONS, along with space, return, etc. Thus the alternative search string for *spoke to* is **\bspoke\Wto\b** (or **\Wspoke\W\to\W**), which is based on non-word characters rather than the word boundary. (It is not necessary to specify word boundaries and search for **\bspoke\b\W\bto\b**; the simpler query above yields the same results.)

You might think about how likely it is that **spoke\Wto** will give the same results. (Certainly, this search string will find all instances of *spoke to*, but it may also snare other strings if the corpus contains phrases such as *spoke together*.)

A solid session reading about regular expressions is not much fun, and here, in particular, time reading this text should be interspersed with generous periods of experimentation. In general, it is best to try out different regex searches, starting with simple searches and increasing the complexity of the expression symbol by symbol. It is also true that regexes created one day look opaque, even to their creator, the next day. Useful regexes should be saved in a file with a descriptive label.

While there is a generally agreed core of regex forms, each software program that includes them has its own idiosyncrasies due to the general context within which the regular expressions operate. Even if you are familiar with regex syntax, you will need to experiment with a variety of options to see how regular expression searches are implemented in *ParaConc*.

[aeiou]　Square brackets are used to indicate choices, as in [eo], which matches one character, *e* or *o*. In addition, it is possible to specify a choice of a set of characters, as in **[0123456789]**, which can be also be given as the range **[0-9]**. Letters and numbers can be specified as **[0-9a-zA-Z]**, but remember that despite the length of this range only one alphanumeric character encountered in the text is matched by this search term; square brackets are always associated with just a single character in the text.

\d \w \D \W　Metacharacters are commonly used in place of the standard ranges. Thus \d is any digit, equivalent to [0-9]. The metacharacter \w is equivalent to any alphanumeric character, but in addition to digits and numbers, it includes characters not listed as word delimiters in SEARCH OPTIONS. Conversely, \D is any non-digit and, as discussed above, \W is any non-alphanumeric.

OR |　Let us return to the question of how regular expressions can be used in a lemma search. One possibility is to use | to indicate logical "or" as in \bspeak\b | \bspeaks\b | \bspoke\b | \bspoken\b etc. In general, parentheses are used to indicate the scope of a disjunction. In this case, however, they are not necessary since strings take precedence over disjunction. (In other words, the first part of the search query specified above is not interpreted as a search for **speak** followed by \b or \b.)

a? = optional a　Another way to perform this lemma search is to specify the query **speaks?** | **spoken?** which includes two kinds of disjunction, | and ?. The question mark is a rather specialised form of disjunction and is typically classified as a counter, which means zero or one instance of the symbol specified. The search string **s?** or **[s]?** stands for *s* or zero (nothing). Other similar forms of counters are s+ and s*, which are equivalent to one or more *s* and zero or more *s*. (Note the difference in the use of * in a simple text search where it is equivalent to zero or more characters and here where it means zero or more instances of the preceding expression—*s* in this case.)

greed	In some situations, searches involving the use of + and * will match a larger than expected chunk of text. This is because these operators match the maximum string possible: a feature known as greediness.
	An alternative search string we could enter is **sp[eo]a?k[se]?n?**, which finds words containing *sp* followed by *e* or *o,* and an optional *a,* followed by *k,* an optional *s* or *e,* and finally, an optional *n*. Since we did not specify a word boundary, the search will also capture *outspokenly* and perhaps exotica (in English texts) such as words like *prospekt*.
lemma	The search string **\bsp[eo]a?k[sei]?n?g?\b** does a good job at capturing the SPEAK lemma, including *speaking*. Since these strings are fairly complex you should definitely take advantage of the fact that, as mentioned above, the previous search strings are available from the drop-down box at the end of the search text box. A separate search term history is maintained for each of the three types of advanced search.
scope	If we wish to search for *speak* followed by either *to* or *with,* and we try the string **speak\Wto\b	\bwith\b**, we will find that we have specified a search for either *with* or *speak to*. To search for *speak to* or *speak with*, we need to specify the scope of the disjunction and use the search term **\bspeak\W(to\b | \bwith\b)**.
while ...	A complex search of a large corpus may take some time. What can you do while the search is progressing? You have several options (in addition to making a cup of coffee). For instance, you can scroll through the hits as they are displayed to start looking for interesting examples. You can also click on a line to see which corpus file it comes from and to see any other information provided in tracked tags. (The information is displayed in the lower left of the window.) Clicking on a line will also allow you to view the larger context for the hit, which is displayed in the upper context window. Finally, you can click on the DETAILS button in the search progress window to check on the search settings in effect.
NOT ^	If you wanted to search for *York*, you might well be overwhelmed by instances of *New York*, even in a British newspaper text. One way to avoid these instances is exclude the word *New*. To accomplish this, we can take advantage of the NOT symbol ^ and use the search string **[^N][^e][^w]\WYork\b** or simply, **[^w]\WYork\b**. If, to continue with our example, you also wanted to exclude instances of the *Duchess of York,* and *Archibishop of York,* then you might disallow both *f* and *w,* as in

[^fw]\WYork\b, although this would also exclude *City of York.*

Turning to another example, perhaps we would like to find examples of *an* followed by a word that does not start with a vowel. To do this, we search for **\ban\W[^aeiouAEIOU].** (Performing this search reveals some interesting results including, in a newspaper text, some errors that have occurred due to the process of writing and revising text. Looking at the results, we find that in some cases *an* turns up when it is separated from a vowel-initial noun by an intervening adjective, as in *an large order.* Presumably an earlier version of the text contained the phrase *an order* and the *an* was not converted to *a* when the adjective *large* was added.)

^ $ anchors The occurrence of **^** as the first item after [means NOT. In other positions outside of square brackets, it will be interpreted as the beginning of a line. The dollar sign $ is the anchor for the end of a line.

\1 same again Let us look at a rather different search query: **\W(is | are)\W\1\W.** The \1 option is essentially a way of repeating whatever is specified in the preceding parentheses. (If there is more than one set of parentheses, then \1, \2, can be used to reference the corresponding groupings.) In this particular example, the expression grouped by parentheses contains a disjunction and the query will match instances of *is is* and *are are.* A simple text search (or two) could replicate this search, but there are searches that would be much more difficult to carry out using a simple text search. For example, if we wish to locate three-word alliterations, that is, sequences of three words starting with the same letter, you could use the simple text query **a* a* a*,** then **b* b* b*,** etc. Or you could use a single regex search: **\W(\w)\w*\W\1\w*\W\1\w*\W.**

{n,m} Does English allow a string of *sss* or *ssss* in a word? Or are all such occurrences likely to be typos and spelling mistakes? We could simply search for **sss,** or we can use a counter—a number enclosed by curly brackets—and search for **s{3}.** If you do this, you might find quite a few typos such as *embarrasssing,* and also some acceptable expressions such as *Yesss!* and *Pssst!* Other formulations of similar search queries are **s{3,5}** to capture *sss, ssss* and *sssss.* And to look for three or more s, we can search for **s{3,}.**

Here is a question. If the word *Psssst!* occurs in a text and you search for **s{3,4},** will the word show up once, twice or three times in the hits? You might think that the hits would be *Psssst! Psssst!* and *Psssst!.* In fact, that there will only be one hit, equivalent to *Psssst!.* This is another example of greediness in action; the search term will only match the maximum string.

perfect search If we wish to search for the English perfect in an untagged corpus, then we know that we have to search for something like *has* or *have* followed by an *-en/-ed* form. This can be accomplished by the following regex search query: **\bha[vs]e?\W\w{4,}e[nd]\b**. The part of the search query that we hope will match the participle is "padded" with alphanumeric characters (**\w**) to eliminate shorter words ending in *-en* or *–ed* such as *ten* and *bed*. However, some good hits such as *seen* will also be omitted by this search query and in cases like this it is up to the user to formulate the search query in such a way as to get the right balance between a good retrieval rate and a high percentage of desired forms in the concordance results. The specification of a minimum of four letters in the participle in the search query above has the effect of increasing the percentage of good "hits" in the results, at the cost of missing some instances of the present perfect that occur in the corpus.

Let us continue with this example and make a modification to the search query to capture cases in which a word intervenes between the auxiliary and participle. Thus, to capture those strings in which an adverb (or *not* or *been*) occurs before the participle, we can add a specification for a word (at least three characters long) **\W\w\w\w+\W** or **\W\w{3,}\W**. The revised search query then becomes **\bha[vs]e?\W\w{3,} \W\w{4,}e[nd]\b**. And, finally, to make the adverb optional we group the "word" characters comprising the intervening word and add a counter: **\bha[vs]e?(\W\w{3,}){0,1}\W\w{4,}e[nd]\b**.

You might try out a broader search query based on the following: **\bha[vs]e?(\W\w+){0,2}\W\w+e[nd]\b**. How do the results compare with those produced by the previous search query?

If you have followed these examples, you will have a sense of the use and power of regular expression searches. I would encourage you to experiment in building up different regex search queries. The language is very powerful and repays some attention to the details of the query syntax. You will need some time to work out the interaction between regexes and other parts of the program. For example, if you are making use of upper case in regex searches, you should make sure that IGNORE CASE OF LETTERS is not checked in the search dialogue box.

For those unsatisfied with the extent of the coverage here, there are several books devoted solely to the elucidation of regular expressions.

The table below summarises regular expression syntax.

.	any character
[a-z]	any lower case letter
[0-9]	any number
[aeuio]	any vowel (in English)
[^lr]	not l or r
\b[a-z]+\b	lower case word
\b[A-Z][a-z]*\b	word with upper case initial letter
\b[0-9]+\b	number
\b	word boundary
\B	word non-boundary
\d	any digit
\D	any non-digit
\w	any word character (= alphanumeric)
\W	any non-word character (defined by word delimiters)
\s	whitespace
\S	non-whitespace
*	zero or more
+	one or more
{n}	n instances of previous expression
{n,m}	from n to m
{n,}	at least n
?	previous expression is optional

4.2 Part of Speech Tags

speech_NNS POS tagging in parallel corpora is still relatively rare, in part due to the problems of tagging languages other than English. It is possible, of course, to tag the English component while leaving the second language untagged,

To take advantage of this specialised annotation, it is necessary to indicate within *ParaConc* the distinction between part-of-speech tags and other tags. Once this is accomplished, the suppress/display options will work and, more importantly, we can perform a word/tag search. Again we select TAG SETTINGS and this time choose PART OF SPEECH TAGS. If the POS tags take a form such as *the_AT*, we select EMBEDDED IN WORD and enter _ in the DELIMITER CHARACTER box. This might be described as "attached to word." The tag is connected directly to the word by a special symbol such as _ or ^, and the end of the tag is typically a space or other word-delimiter character.

If the tags are specified, as in different versions of the *BNC* as *<w AT>the*, then we select OUTSIDE WORD (see Figure 5) and enter <w and <c (for punctuation) in TAG START and > in TAG END. These tags, which may or may not be attached to the word, have an explicit tag end (although it would be possible to use # meaning "space" as the tag end, but this would not cover line returns, etc.) In addition, since in this particular example the tag precedes the word it classifies, we must select the BEFORE WORD box.

Figure 26: Defining POS tags and meta-tags

If you are using other corpora, then the BEFORE WORD box would perhaps be unchecked and the special punctuation tags <c > omitted.

4.3 Tag Search

A corpus in which each word is annotated with part-of-speech tags provides a richer, more structured database allowing targetted searches and opening up the possibility of performing syntactic (or colligational) analyses.

It is possible to investigate a tagged corpus using a simple TEXT SEARCH or a REGULAR EXPRESSION search and in this case the search queries simply treat both the words and their tags as searchable strings of symbols. There may well be good reasons for carrying out such a search, but here we will focus on searching tagged corpora using a TAG SEARCH.

Before initiating a TAG SEARCH, information on the format of the different tags must be entered in the Part of Speech TAG SETTINGS and the SCAN CORPUS routine must have been run.

To perform a TAG SEARCH, select ADVANCED SEARCH from the CONCORDANCE menu. Once the ADVANCED SEARCH dialogue box appears, select the TAG SEARCH radio button in the SEARCH SYNTAX section on the left of the dialogue box, as shown in Figure 22.

old&JJ   The search query in a TAG SEARCH can contain any permutation of words, tags, or words and tags. The basic syntax of the search query is **word&tag**. Note that this is the case whatever the ordering of words and tags in the corpus itself as all details about corpus format were specified in TAG SETTINGS.

The & is used as a special symbol to distinguish specifications of words from specifications of tags. If an alternative symbol such as $ is preferred, then simply substitute $ for & in the TAG SEARCH SEPARATOR text box in SEARCH OPTIONS. (See Figure 27.)

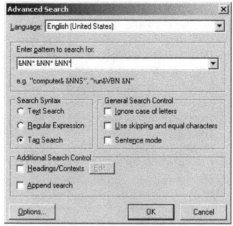

Figure 27: A Tag Search

4.4 Searching for Words and Tags

Having a tagged corpus opens up a lot of possibilities. We can look for different constructions, as described below, and in searching for words, we can pinpoint with considerable accuracy the forms we are interested in.

In English, in particular, there is a considerable amount of zero derivation, i.e., a lack of morphology, which means that many words have the same form whether they are verbs or nouns. Thus, while *hold* most frequently occurs as a verb, it is also a noun, as in *ship's hold*. Having a tagged corpus makes it much easier to locate the desired POS, and this becomes particularly important when we want to search for the rarer of the two forms. For instance, we can search for the noun *hold* by entering **hold&NN1** as a search term. If we want to find the plural noun form *holds*, we can use the search query **holds&NN2**.

wildcards ? % What if we want to search for both singular and plural noun forms? In this case, we can make use of the simple wildcard characters % ? * and enter the search query **hold%&NN?** or **hold%&NN***.

case sensitive Note that if IGNORE CASE OF LETTERS is left unchecked, then the search for tags will be case sensitive.

So far I have emphasised the positive aspects of working with a tagged corpus. However, once the search is completed, a disadvantage of a tagged corpus is only too clearly evident in the cluttered appearance of the search results. Now that we have used the tags to refine our search, we will probably want to hide the POS tags, and perhaps the normal tags too, before examining the results in detail. To achieve this, select SUPPRESS in the DISPLAY menu and choose first PART OF SPEECH and then reselect SUPPRESS and select TAGS. All the mark-up will disappear and you will then be left with only the words. The idea is to have the best of both worlds: to exploit the tags in the search process and then suppress them when the results are obtained.

Whether the mark-up in the concordance results window is displayed or hidden, the collocate frequency and sorting functions will always ignore the tags and work solely on the words. (To avoid this state of affairs, it would be necessary to prevent the collection of the tag identifier information by the COLLECT TAG INFORMATION routine.)

As mentioned above, one advantage of a tagged corpus is the possibility of looking for examples of lexical/ syntactic units such as the *way* construction, as illustrated by *muddle our way through* or *fight his way out*. To locate these constructions, we need to specify the sequence of verb, possessive pronoun and *way*, i.e., **&VV* &APPGE way&**.

wildcard @	The search query given above finds three-word instances of the *way* construction based on Verb + Pronoun + *way*, but perhaps this is too restrictive. If we want to allow for the possibility of "intervening words" occurring in this construction, we can make use of the 'range' wildcard character @. We can set the range of @ in SEARCH OPTIONS to be 0 to 1, which means zero or one intervening words, and then search for **&VV* @ &APPGE @ way&.** As it turns out, we only get a few extra examples, in which, for example, *own* occurs before *way*.
* alone	Let us look at one final variant. If we wanted to find examples in which there is exactly one word intervening between the pronoun and *way*, we could use the special character * and search for **&VV* &APPGE * way&**

4.5 Searching for Part of Speech Tags

To create a search query that locates complex noun-noun compounds consisting of five nouns, we can search for **&NN? &NN? &NN? &NN? &NN?.**

To take another example of a search for a syntactic form, we can look in the corpus for infinitive plus present participle constructions. To do this, we can enter something like the search query **&TO &VVI &VVG.** (Naturally, the corpus has to be tagged for POS for these searches to work.) The results of this search will typically show a variety of verbs being used, with the most common being *start*, as in *to start talking*, with the phrase *to stop x-ing* being much rarer. The verbs *keep* and *continue* also occur, giving us a class of verbs that focus on the initiation, continuation and completion of actions. Another common verb is *go* and not surprisingly there might be some fixed expressions such as *to go shopping* found in the corpus.

4.6 Searching for Words

ignoring tags It is simple to search for words in a tagged corpus. One way to do this is to enter the search words and &, as in **take& part&.** By default, however, you can, in fact, simply search for **take part**, without specifying the word-tag boundary explicitly. Thus, if you have a tagged corpus and you want to simply ignore the presence of tags, you just enter the words or phrase you wish to locate. (Note: this will only work in the TAG SEARCH option.)

4.7 Meta-tags

In the above searches, we made use of wildcard characters to capture a range of tags in the search. For example, we used the search term **NN?** to capture the tags for both singular and plural nouns, NN1 and NN2. However, the search query **NN?** also matches the tag NNB, which is used for titles such as *Mr., Lady,* and *General*. What we need is a way to specify a tag representation that covers singular and plural nouns but not titles.

define a tagset To do this, we can create a meta-tag CNOUN, which we define in the meta-tags section. We choose TAG SETTINGS from the file menu, select PART OF SPEECH TAGS and in the META-TAGS part of the dialogue box, choose ADD. Enter the name of the new meta-tag (i.e., CNOUN) and enter all the constituent tags (i.e, NN1, NN2), separated by a comma in the TAGS box. Note: In defining the tags making up a meta-tag, it is permissible to include wildcard characters in order to capture more than one tag name. Meta-meta-tags are not allowed, however; you can only use actual tags in the definition of a meta-tag.

The use of meta-tags allows the user to build on the tagset of the corpus to define a new tagset to be used in search queries. Say, for instance, that we wish to define a tag complementizer that includes *who, whom, which* and *that*, which may be tagged as, respectively PNQS, PNQO, DDQ, and CST. It is very easy to define a new tag COMP that covers all four original tags. Once this is done, searches can be carried out using the overarching category COMP or a specific (original) category such as PNQS.

4.8 Searching for Punctuation

The *BNC* contains tags for punctuation as well as tags for words. The punctuation tags have the form <c PUNC> and in the settings for PART OF SPEECH TAGS we entered both <w and <c as valid tag starts. Based on these punctuation tags, we could look for three-word sentences using the query **&YSTP * * * &YSTP**.

Note: Since the full stops (periods) will belong to different sentences, we need to ensure that SENTENCE MODE in the ADVANCED SEARCH dialogue box is not selected. In addition, even though we are searching for tags indicating full stops, we need to remove the full stop from the set of word delimiters specified in SEARCH OPTIONS.

4.9 Parallel Search

One kind of search tailored for use with parallel texts is a parallel search, which is an option in the SEARCH menu. This option allows you to constrain your search based on occurrences in the different parallel texts. The search dialogue box is shown in Figure 28.

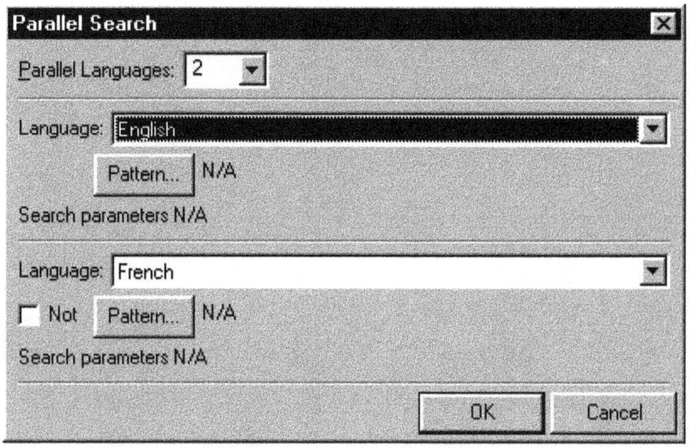

Figure 28: Parallel search

Clicking on the Pattern box under Language: English brings up the normal advanced search dialogue box and a search query can be entered. In this case, we can enter a word such as **without**. We can then move to Language: French and again click on Pattern and enter another search string such as **sans**. This type of search is particularly useful for providing general information on the degree and nature of congruence between two candidate expressions (Barlow 2008. See also Varadi and Liss 2001). The steps involved as follows:

   (i) perform a parallel search for word1-trans1 and examine the usage and
      collocations for word1 and trans1;

   (ii) perform a parallel search for word1-NOT trans1 and again examine the
      usage of word1;
   (iii) switch language and repeat the procedure.

The data from these searches can be used to get an idea which meanings and uses of word1 translate into trans1 and which meanings and uses don't translate into trans1. Before undertaking the steps outlined above, we can obtain a general idea of formal equivalence by performing a simple text search for *without* and checking the number of occurrences of *sans*. In the parallel corpus examined here, we find around 11,000 instances of *without* are associated with 9,000 instances of *sans* and so there seems to be a reasonably congruent relationship. For more detailed information, we can look at the collocate frequency information, shown in Figure 29, which displays the collocate information for *without* and *sans* side by side.

ParaConc - Frenwrk - [Frequency Statistics - All]

File Search Frequency Display Window Info

English (United States) - [without] | French (Standard) - [sans]

English (United States) - [without]

2-Left		1-Left		1-Right		2-Right	
633	the	638	and	950	any	883	the
590	be	424	goes	949	the	533	to
421	it	244	that	735	a	456	that
371	to	220	is	464	saying	396	and
336	of	191	but	398	delay	200	a
278	and	112	do	254	having	191	in
238	a	103	not	234	doubt	184	any
233	this	101	or	205	being	156	being
179	in	99	europe	139	which	145	it
164	is	96	possible	114	taking	135	doubt
124	european	87	union	113	this	133	for
117	with	73	so	105	exception	130	or
116	that	72	this	100	prejudice	128	we
112	no	70	achieved	94	an	110	of
95	been	69	-	93	it	98	i
95	not	68	television	89	frontiers	87	into
94	for	67	it	88	further	83	having
88	cannot	67	states	79	even	82	this
87	their	65	even	73	making	79	directive
82	are	64	because	69	their	74	there
81	do	63	countries	58	its	66	need
76	can	57	place	57	them	61	on
65	member	56	market	56	going	61	support
65	on	56	people	54	however	55	is
56	these	55	policy	52	discriminat...	55	with
49	being	53	are	52	waiting	53	mr
49	our	50	be	48	losing	52	an
48	all	50	done	47	giving	51	as
48	have	48	work	46	borders	50	from
47	an	44	world	46	trial	47	european

French (Standard) - [sans]

2-Left		1-Left		1-Right		2-Right	
672	de	286	et	424	que	558	de
364	la	215	que	268	la	328	les
274	des	147	mais	230	aucun	308	et
231	être	146	va	192	le	275	la
228	le	87	télévision	191	une	262	le
225	et	86	européenne	182	avoir	195	que
212	en	81	en	165	dire	194	en
182	à	79	pas	153	frontières	193	à
179	les	76	ou	148	les	175	des
144	il	74	faire	141	pour	144	doute
132	se	71	est	128	être	134	autant
125	du	61	car	110	un	121	sans
124	une	60	-	106	devoir	120	il
117	pas	57	europe	93	délai	108	nous
103	ce	52	membres	81	exception	102	pour
101	cette	51	pays	64	attendre	99	moindre
98	un	46	même	64	débat	95	dans
92	été	44	européen	63	en	84	du
87	avec	41	commission	62	même	81	cela
77	est	41	qui	61	plus	74	un
65	ces	40	ce	61	tenir	71	une
64	directive	32	démocratie	59	doute	60	au
60	plus	32	sécurité	59	se	59	ce
54	leur	31	cela	56	toutefois	59	compte
54	états	31	leur	54	préjudice	59	je
47	au	31	paix	52	faire	59	par
47	nous	31	au	52	qu'il	54	soutien
47	sont	29	monde	52	fait	53	sur
46	l'	28	fait	51	porter	44	aucune
45	peut	27	impossible	50	prendre		
		26	lieu				

375 parallel files loaded   20,386,783 / 21,174,984

Figure 29: The collocates of without *and* sans

By scanning the data, we can see that the most common left collocate is *and* and *et*, indicating a general similarity of usage of *without* and *sans*. Looking at Figure 29, we also see the progressive *–ing* forms following *without* in English and we find that *sans que* and *sans frontieres* stand out as not having obvious equivalents. Going back to the concordance lines, we discover that *sans frontiers,* for example, is associated with *without frontiers, without borders* and *without limits*. Carrying out a parallel search for **without NOT sans** and looking at the collocate frequency list for *without* we obtain the results in the table shown in Figure 30. From this we observe the presence of the idiom *goes without saying,* which in the French segments is often rendered as *il va de soi que.*

2-Left		1-Left		1-Right		2-Right	
239	it	268	goes	292	saying	233	that
119	be	123	and	197	a	175	the
99	the	99	is	187	delay	126	to
92	to	93	do	175	the	75	and
67	of	45	not	173	any	73	doubt
62	and	45	that	149	doubt	60	a
58	is	40	but	38	having	47	in
50	that	28	people	36	further	38	it
48	this	26	be	33	this	37	we
41	a	24	are	30	being	29	for
38	cannot	24	go	30	it	29	of
35	in	18	even	25	its	28	being
33	can	18	up	25	which	25	any
30	are	16	europe	24	prejudice	25	i
27	not	16	will	22	an	23	or
22	with	15	countries	21	exception	22	this
20	european	15	left	20	their	19	ado
18	for	15	so	18	that	19	but
16	do	14	it	18	them	19	there
15	all	14	work	17	such	18	as
15	been	13	achieved	16	access	17	an
15	these	13	place	15	regard	17	mr
14	should	13	those	13	these	14	so
14	which	12	.	12	fail	13	european
13	being	12	done	12	going	13	is
12	an	12	which	12	question	12	our
12	have	11	or	12	reference	12	with

375 parallel files loaded   20,386,783 / 21,174,984

Figure 30: Collocates of without *(not associated with* sans*)*

Searching for **sans** we find 22,000 instances of *sans* associated with 10,000 hits for *without*. If we perform a parallel search for **sans NOT without** and use the Hot Words or the Translation utility, we obtain English words such as *undoubtably, unreservedly, unprecedented, unequivocally*, and *defenceless*, which provides indication as to the type of equivalences involved.

5. Word Lists, Collocates and Frequency Lists

Summary: To create a word list, select CORPUS FREQUENCY DATA from the FREQUENCY menu and choose alphabetical or frequency order. The collocates of a search word can be calculated by the program. It is also possible to use the ADVANCED COLLOCATION option to produce a frequency list of collocations larger than two words The parameters controlling the results are listed in FREQUENCY OPTIONS.

word list

It is sometimes instructive to destroy the structure of a text in order to reveal patterns hidden by the normal linear arrangement. The most radical transformation of a text used in linguistic analyses is to rip it apart to produce a word list. Creating a word list involves snipping the text at particular places, typically the spaces between words, and counting the resulting tokens. Even if the software produces the word list on the execution of the relevant command, it is important to be aware of the existence of choices made in performing this transformation, as well as of the uses that can be made of the transformed text. (See Section 10.7 for a detailed discussion on the definition of words.)

Transforming a text into list of words removes the context for individual words, which means that all the linear context, i.e., all syntagmatic information, is eliminated. Consequently, it is not possible to use a word list to analyse how the information in the text is presented, but it can give an idea of what information is in the text and, of course, what words are in the text.

The most frequent words in a corpus are grammatical or function words. Each sentence contains such words, but content words , in contrast, differ from one sentence to the next. Typically, the most frequent content words in a corpus are of interest since they give the best indication of the nature of the corpus. If a corpus is being analysed to discover something about English and French usage, then we might want to know what the most frequent 1000 words are; what the next most frequent 1000 words are, and so on.

5.1 Frequency Options

Choosing FREQUENCY OPTIONS allows the frequency list to be tailored to fit particular requirements. It is possible to limit the data presented in three main ways, as can be seen from the FREQUENCY AND COLLOCATION OPTIONS dialogue box. First, we can set the maximum number of lines in the frequency list (using the MAXIMUM LINES parameter), which means that it is a simple matter to find, for example, the twenty most frequent words or the hundred most frequent words in a corpus. For creating normal frequency lists, it is best to set this number to 98000. Secondly, a lower frequency boundary can be selected (MINIMUM FREQUENCY).

The third main option is to set an upper frequency boundary (MAXIMUM FREQUENCY) that excludes words occurring more often than the set threshold. (The setting of 0 is used to indicate no upper boundary.)

With these parameters, it is possible to examine various frequency lists for a corpus. The most common uses are to list the most frequent words or, alternatively, to display those words that occur just once.

The two checkboxes in the dialogue box (IGNORE CASE OF LETTERS and SKIP TAGS) control case-sensitivity and tag-sensitivity in frequency calculations.

Important note: These options must be set for each language.

5.2 Stop List

Because grammatical or function words such as *the* are both of high frequency and generally not very interesting, it is often desirable to omit them and concentrate on words of interest which might otherwise be masked by the more frequent forms.

exclude

There are two ways to exclude a set of words from consideration. One option is to create and load a text-only file containing the words to be excluded from the frequency listings—a stop list. The second is to add words to the stop list from within the program. Both these functions are accessed via FREQUENCY OPTIONS. To exclude a particular set of words from the frequency counts, select CONTENT WORDS ONLY, then choose EDIT, and type in the words to be omitted, Alternatively, you can load a file containing the words you wish to exclude from the frequency counts. (The words should be listed one to a line in the file.)

The various frequency settings can be individually tailored for each of the languages selected.

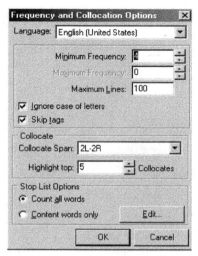

Figure 29: Frequency and collocation options

The word list can be created for any of the languages loaded. See Figure 30.

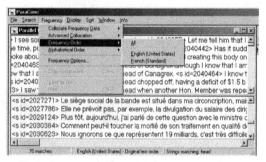

Figure 30: Corpus frequency commands

The results will be something like those shown in Figure 31, with for each language the word count, the percentage of the word compared with the number of word tokens, and the word itself.

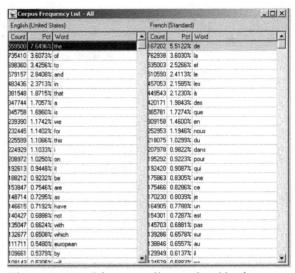

Figure 31: Word frequency lists, ordered by frequency

The list can be ordered alphabetically as in Figure 32, although the side-by-side display is misleading in the sense that the two lists are not linked. (If the list obtained looks odd because it contains only numbers, then you will need to set the Max number of lines parameter in FREQUENCY OPTIONS for that language to many more than the default 100.)

Alphabetical Word List – All

\	English (United States)			French (Standard)	
Count	Pct	Word	Count	Pct	Word
10	0.0000%	able-bodied	342	0.0016%	abordée
28	0.0001%	ably	264	0.0012%	abordées
16	0.0001%	abm	388	0.0018%	abordés
33	0.0002%	abnormal	53	0.0003%	abou
9	0.0000%	abnormalities	350	0.0017%	abouti
17	0.0001%	abnormally	12	0.0001%	aboutie
14	0.0001%	aboard	8	0.0000%	abouties
419	0.0021%	abolish	726	0.0034%	aboutir
388	0.0019%	abolished	96	0.0005%	aboutira
28	0.0001%	abolishes	42	0.0002%	aboutirait
249	0.0012%	abolishing	8	0.0000%	aboutirions
524	0.0026%	abolition	27	0.0001%	aboutirons
8	0.0000%	abolitionist	45	0.0002%	aboutiront
36	0.0002%	abominable	9	0.0000%	aboutissait
13	0.0001%	abomination	24	0.0001%	aboutissant
8	0.0000%	aboriginal	18	0.0001%	aboutissants
10	0.0000%	aborted	93	0.0004%	aboutisse
436	0.0021%	abortion	47	0.0002%	aboutissement
93	0.0005%	abortions	84	0.0004%	aboutissent
11	0.0001%	abortive	19	0.0001%	aboutissions
16	0.0001%	abound	14	0.0001%	aboutissons
33291	0.1633%	about	142	0.0007%	aboutit
14	0.0001%	about-turn	11	0.0001%	abraham
4297	0.0211%	above	48	0.0002%	abri
9	0.0000%	above-average	15	0.0001%	abris
95	0.0004%	above-mentioned	17	0.0001%	abritant

Figure 32: Word frequency lists – alphabetical order

The program provides other information that can be used in various frequency-based calculations.

 The frequency of the keyword is given by the total number of hits—assuming, of course, that the whole corpus was searched and the search did not end prematurely. In any case, even with an incomplete search it may still be possible to estimate the total frequency of the search word in the corpus by observing the percentage of the corpus that was scanned before the search ended.

5.3 Collocate Frequencies

ParaConc furnishes a variety of frequency statistics, but the two main kinds are corpus frequency and collocate frequency. The command CORPUS FREQUENCY DATA creates a word list for the whole corpus, as described in Chapter 5. Choosing COLLOCATE FREQUENCY DATA from the FREQUENCY menu (or CTRL-F) displays the collocates of the search term ranked in terms of frequency.

frequency

The collocates of a word are its frequent neighbouring words. In *ParaConc,* the collocate frequency calculations are tied to a particular search word and so the frequency menu only appears once a search has been performed. Typically, the collocation data produced by the COLLOCATE FREQUENCY DATA command is organised in four columns, with one column for each position surrounding the keyword: 2nd left, 1st left, 1st right and 2nd right. (Thus 1st left refers to the word before the search term and 1st right refers to the word following the search term.) The columns show the collocates in descending order of frequency. This describes the collocate frequencies for a span 2L-2R. The span and other information is controlled by the settings in frequency options, as shown in Figure 29. The collocate frequency span can range from 1L-1R to 4L-4R.

Returning to the earlier example of a search for *head* in English (and an associated search for *tête* in French), we can see the words commonly occurring with the search word by scrolling through the concordance lines. Conveniently, we can make the program display the frequency of particular collocates for both *head* and *tête* or either one by selecting COLLOCATE FREQUENCY DATA from the FREQUENCY menu and choosing either ALL, ENGLISH or FRENCH, as shown in Figure 33.

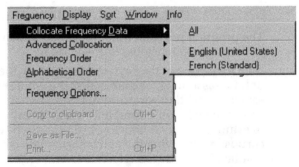

Figure 33: Collocate frequency in multiple languages

The program then calculates, for the language chosen the frequency of collocates surrounding the search term for a particular span (Figure 34)

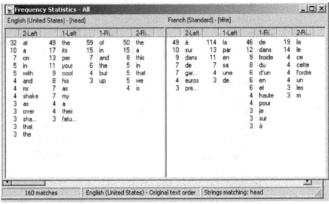

Figure 34: The collocates of head *and* tête

Firth

The usefulness of collocate frequencies in providing information of various kinds should not be underestimated. The linguist J.R. Firth is often quoted as saying that you shall know a word by the company it keeps. The ramifications of this statement made in the 1950s are still being explored today. (See, for example, *Text and Corpus Analysis* by Michael Stubbs, *Patterns and Meanings* by Alan Partington and *Corpus Collocation Concordance* by John Sinclair.) Corpus analysts tend, in one way or another, to explore the extent to which the formal and semantic properties of a word are reflected in its collocates.

Let's look briefly at a simple investigation to explore the role of collocations as a guide to meaning. The words *wide* and *broad* will suffice as an example of a pair of words that can be described as synonymous. Synonyms, words having the same meaning, might reasonably be expected to show up with the same collocates since these would be equally compatible with either of the synonyms. On the other hand, differences in the range and frequency of collocates occurring with each of the two synonyms may be used to provide clues to subtle differences in meaning. An examination of the set of collocates of a word provides some evidence about meaning, a domain that is generally agreed to be difficult to investigate and for which it is hard to find empirical data.

We can perform searches for *broad* and *wide* and examine the collocates of each word. The most frequent left and right collocates of *broad* and *wide* are given in Figures 35 and 36.

648	a		253	consensus
620	the		207	economic
132	very		152	support
77	is		130	guidelines
40	in		101	majority
33	as		92	agreement
28	this		70	range
27	and		69	and
26	too		48	debate
25	of		33	sense
18	be		33	spectrum
17	these		30	political
17	with		29	public
14	its		27	outlines
14	on		25	a
13	for		22	lines
13	such		21	terms
11	our		20	consultation
9	extremely		17	coalition
9	was		17	in
8	have		17	international
8	so		16	thrust
8	sufficiently		15	definition
8	that		13	principles

*Figure 35: Left and right collocates of **broad***

379	a		256	range
89	the		65	variety
49	very		44	open
23	as		39	support
23	too		23	and

20	and		18	consensus
17	is		16	public
15	door		15	a
12	this		12	consultation
11	so		12	debate
9	how		12	spectrum
8	received		12	to
8	to		10	scope
8	with		9	majority
8	world		9	the
6	extremely		7	area
6	increasingly		7	as
5	open		7	of
5	over		7	ranging
4	already		6	an
4	are		6	diversity
4	such		5	agreement
3	attracted		5	areas
3	doors		5	definition

*Figure 36: Left and right collocates of **wide***

Examining the results, we find that *wide* can have an adverbial, as well as adjectival function with the result that the left collocates of the two words are somewhat different. If we compare the right collocates for the two words, we see that *area, range, spectrum* and *support* occur with both *broad* and *wide*, indicating their similarity in meaning, but other right collocates are not shared by the two words. Examining the words that collocate with only one of the pair of words should provide some clues to the differences in meaning of the two synonyms. Taking this approach, we can omit words such as *range* and just list those right collocates that occur with only one of the synonyms. Here we ignore frequency data and simply compare the two lists of words looking for clues to the nature of the differences between the two synonyms. The first few examples from a list of collocates unique to each word are shown in Figure 37.

broad	*wide*
acceptance	access

action	berth
agenda	choice
aim	circulation
alliance	discrepancy
approach	disparity
approval	distribution
autonomy	divergence
backing	diversity
basis	exchange

*Figure 37: Some unique collocates of **broad** and **wide***

Objects can be broad or wide, leading to the similarities in meaning, but *wide* can also be used to describe the distance between two points and we see that aspect of the meaning showing up in *wide discrepancy, wide disparity* etc. When we examine the French translations, we see that *large* is a common equivalent for *wide* and *broad*, but not in *wide discrepancy* type of meanings.

re-calculate

Note: The COLLOCATE FREQUENCY DATA command can only be chosen when a concordance results window is active. Note also that if you want to force a recalculation of the collocate frequencies, you must first close the COLLOCATE FREQUENCY DATA window. Thus, you must be careful about choosing the COLLOCATE FREQUENCY DATA command after having deleted some concordance lines. If no collocate window tied to the concordance is open, then the collocates will be (re-)calculated and everything will be fine, but if a collocate window already exists, then the COLLOCATE FREQUENCY DATA command will simply bring up the existing collocates window, the contents of which will not reflect the current state of the concordance results.

5.4 Highlighting Collocations

The software allows potential collocates of the searchword to be highlighted within the concordance results window. This is one way of illustrating frequency information when viewing the concordance lines.

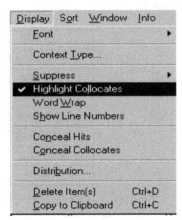

Figure 34: Turning on collocate highlighting

The span of the collocates is set in FREQUENCY OPTIONS, as is the depth of ranking of collocates that are to be highlighted. For example, the 5 most frequent collocates for each position in the span might be highlighted. It is also possible to use the stoplist in FREQUENCY OPTIONS to exclude certain words.

5.5 Advanced Collocation

collocations

One disadvantage of the simple collocate frequency table is that it is not possible to gauge the frequency of collocations consisting of three or more words. To calculate the frequency of these larger chunks, it is necessary to choose ADVANCED COLLOCATION from the FREQUENCY menu and select one or more languages.

The ADVANCED COLLOCATION dialogue box (like ADVANCED SORT) is divided into three sections. The top part of the dialogue box associated with ADVANCED COLLOCATION allows the user to choose from up to three word positions. See Figure 35. The middle part of the dialogue box is labelled Customised Collocation. When checked, this option allows the user to enter word positions (1L,0,1R) defining the collocation into a text box. The user can list positions separated by commas or enter a range of words such as 2L-2R. The lower part, span, will calculate the frequency of chunks containing the searchword without regard for the position of the searchword in the chunk.

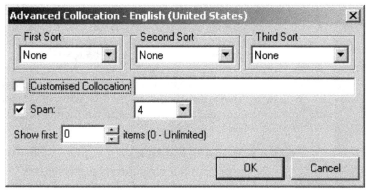

Figure 35: Advanced Collocation dialogue box

The calculation and display of collocations is guided by the settings in FREQUENCY AND COLLOCATION options. See Figure 29.) This dialogue box is invoked by selecting FREQUENCY OPTIONS from the FREQUENCY menu.

The four-word chunks containing the word *broad* are show in Figure 36.

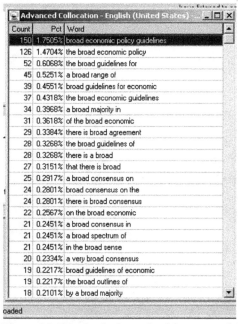

Count	Pct	Word
150	1.7505%	broad economic policy guidelines
126	1.4704%	the broad economic policy
52	0.6068%	the broad guidelines for
45	0.5251%	a broad range of
39	0.4551%	broad guidelines for economic
37	0.4318%	the broad economic guidelines
34	0.3968%	a broad majority in
31	0.3618%	of the broad economic
29	0.3384%	there is broad agreement
28	0.3268%	the broad guidelines of
28	0.3268%	there is a broad
27	0.3151%	that there is broad
25	0.2917%	a broad consensus on
24	0.2801%	broad consensus on the
24	0.2801%	there is broad consensus
22	0.2567%	on the broad economic
21	0.2451%	a broad consensus in
21	0.2451%	a broad spectrum of
21	0.2451%	in the broad sense
20	0.2334%	a very broad consensus
19	0.2217%	broad guidelines of economic
19	0.2217%	the broad outlines of
18	0.2101%	by a broad majority

Figure 36: Results for broad *with a span of 4*

count

The ADVANCED COLLOCATION option can also be used to count the different components making up the search term.

The main collocate frequency table always ignores the search term, which means that if you use wildcard characters or tags in the search query and capture a variety of words as hits, then you need a way to count the different words. You can do this by using ADVANCED COLLOCATION and selecting SEARCH TERM in one column and setting the other two columns to NONE. The ADVANCED COLLOCATION routine will then calculate the frequency of each of the search term forms.

5.6 Saving and Printing the Frequency Results

The output from the frequency analyses can be saved to a file by choosing SAVE AS FILE from the FREQUENCY menu. The frequency file that is active—the collocate frequency or the corpus frequency—will be saved to a text file. The frequency results can be printed using CTRL-P or PRINT. Once again, it is the frequency file that is active that will be printed. It is also possible to copy and paste the frequency results.

6. Working With A Corpus

Summary: Check the configurations in TAG SETTINGS in the FILE menu and then choose LOAD CORPUS FILE(S).

In order for the software to take advantage of the information encoded in texts it is often preferable to enter descriptions of the form of annotations before initiating the loading of files. The following description might seem to be somewhat involved, but once the settings are entered, then the processing and display of the corpora and the search results will be much clearer. In addition, the use of "workspaces," which are described in the next section, is a good way to ensure that the information about the annotations used in the corpus only has to be entered once.

6.1 Aligning the Corpora

If the corpus files are not pre-aligned, select the NOT ALIGNED option. If the files use headings or indicate paragraph boundaries in a particular way, this information will be needed for the alignment. In order to enter this formatting information, select FORMAT (for each language). The FORMAT buttons can be seen in Figs 4 and 5.

format of files   The content of the format dialogue box is shown in Figure 6. The information in the dialogue box is divided into three sections: Headings, Paragraphs, and Sentences, allowing the formatting of each type of text unit to be specified. Thus, in the paragraph section the user can choose from the following:

New Line delimited

HTML/SGML Markers

Two New Lines Delimited

Indented

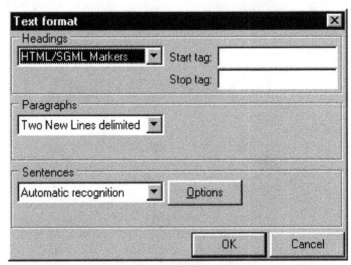

Figure 37: Specifying the format of headings, paragraphs and sentences

<dl>
<dt>Headings</dt>
<dd>

The formatting options for Headings are more complex because the range of options is greater. Some texts may use HTML/SGML tags to mark headings and in this case the form of the tags can be entered. If both the Start tag and End tag are empty the whole text is taken to consist of a single heading.

The sequence %d used to specify HTML/SGML Headings matches any number and so if H%d and /H%d are entered for the Start and End tags, then the program will recognize <H1> ... </H1>, <H2> .... </H2> etc.

Another option is Pattern. The program looks for this specified pattern at the beginning of every paragraph and if it is found, then a new heading is started. The sequence %d means any number; %r means any roman number.

The third option is Regular expression: The program looks for the regular expression at the beginning of every paragraph and, again, if it is found then a new heading is started.
</dd>

<dt>Sentences</dt>
<dd>

The two options that the user can specify for the recognition of Sentences are HTML/SGML or Automatic Recognition.

Note that alignment can only be carried out on two strands (languages) at a time.

ParaConc uses the information about headings to attempt to align the documents at the level of headings (sections) and the user can then make adjustments by merging/splitting sections, as appropriate. Once this is
</dd>
</dl>

done, it is possible to go through the document again aligning the parallel files at the paragraph level. Sentence level alignment, if it is not indicated by SGML tags, is performed using the Gale-Church algorithm (Gale and Church, 1993). After this process, the user goes through the files one more time to make sure that the sentence alignment is satisfactory.

Once the alignment algorithm is successful, then the files will be processed and the menu bar will be expand to include SEARCH and FREQUENCY commands. However, it is a good idea to check the alignment, whether or not the alignment process seems to be successful. To do this, choose VIEW CORPUS FILES from the FILE menu, select a pair of files and click on ALIGNMENT, as in Figure 38.

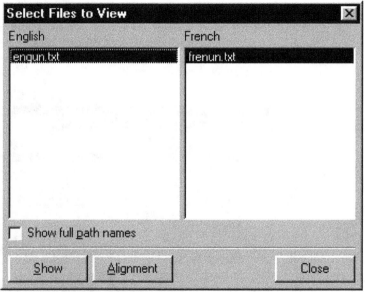

Figure 38: Viewing alignment

The alignment of headings or paragraphs or sentences can be viewed by selecting the appropriate command from the ALIGNMENT menu. (See Figure 39.)

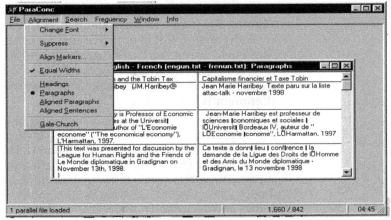

Figure 39: Alignment menu and display of aligned units

In order to make the alignment as clear as possible, the alignment units are indicated by horizontal lines and the sentences within a larger unit follow a colour sequence, as can be seen from Figure 40.

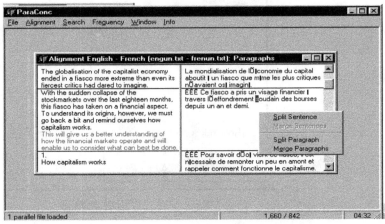

Figure 40: Merging and splitting alignment units

The left mouse button can be used to insert a marker and clicking on the right mouse button brings up a menu of options which allow the splitting or merger of alignment units.

Because some items such as dates or cognates will usually occur in equivalent alignment segments in translated texts, this fact can be used to highlight potential misalignments. The information is not used in the alignment algorithms themselves; it is only used to help the user check the alignment. These equivalences are entered as ALIGNMENT MARKERS SETTINGS, as seen in Figure 41.

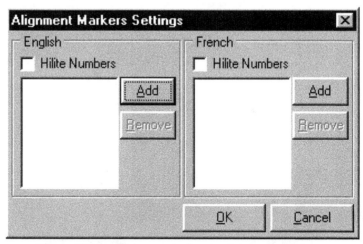

Figure 41: Specifying equivalences: dates or cognates

Important note: If the texts are not pre-aligned and alignment is done within the program, then that alignment information must be saved. This can be accomplished by saving the current files/settings as a workspace. To do this, use the SAVE WORKSPACE command. A safer alternative is to export the aligned corpus.

Alignment can also be achieved with other utilities such as vanilla aligner and WinAlign.

7. Using Workspaces

Summary: Saving a workspace avoids the need to reload (and realign) corpus files or re-process the corpus.

Reloading

As is clear from the previous section, loading and processing a parallel corpus can take some time. Since the same sets of corpus files are often loaded each time *ParaConc* is started, it makes sense to freeze the current state of the program, at will, and return to that state at any time. This is the idea behind a workspace. A workspace is saved as a special ParaConc Workspace file (.pws), which can then be opened at any time to restore *ParaConc* to its previous state, with the corpus loaded ready for searching. Searches and frequency data are, however, not included in the saved workspace. (Only the search histories are saved.)

7.1 Saving a Workspace

A workspace—the current corpus and settings of *ParaConc*—can be saved at any time by selecting the command SAVE WORKSPACE or SAVE WORKSPACE AS from the FILE menu. The usual dialogue box appears and the name and location of the workspace file can be specified in the normal way. (With the possible exception of web documents, it is only the links to the corpus that are saved, not a copy of the corpus itself.)

options

Once a (memorable, descriptive) filename for the saved workspace has been entered, the user is asked to choose some different workspace options. The line/page and the tracked tag info can be saved as part of the workspace. (The saved workspace consists of a saved file and an associated folder of the same name.)

If the corpus consists of downloaded URLs, then selecting the third option in this dialogue box saves the actual contents of the corpus, which avoids the need to reload web documents.

Warning: Keep corpus files and workspace files separate.

It is advisable to create a folder (called Workspaces) to hold all the workspace files (and their associated folders). This will make it easy to locate any given workspace file and avoid mixing of workspace files and corpus files. The first few lines of the workspace file are similar to the following:

[GeneralConfiguration]
CorpusPath=C:\barlow\New Folder\
StopListPath=
ConcordancePath=C:\
[[FreqPath]]=
CorpusFreqPath=
CorpusFont=System,-12,1,-2147483640,0
SystemFont=MS Sans Serif,8,0,-2147483640,0
Language=1033
SaveOnExit=1

If something like this appears in your loaded corpus, then you know that you have loaded a workspace file as a corpus file by mistake. Also if there is a problem opening the workspace, then the CorpusPath attribute may give a clue to files that have been moved.

Once a workspace has been opened, then the user has a choice of two commands: SAVE WORKSPACE AS or simply SAVE WORKSPACE.

SAVE ON EXIT   In addition, the SAVE ON EXIT command can be selected in order to save the current workspace when the user quits the program.

7.2 Opening a Workspace

It is possible to choose OPEN WORKSPACE from the FILE menu (or select CTRL-O) in order to load a saved workspace file. If OPEN WORKSPACE is activated when corpus files have been loaded, then those files are unloaded and replaced by the corpus specified in the workspace file.

shortcut   Hint: A quick way to open *ParaConc* with the corpus loaded is to double-click on a saved workspace file.

8. Displaying The Results

Summary: Moving from one window to another is accomplished by selecting the desired location from the list in the WINDOW menu or by clicking on the appropriate window. The format of concordance lines can be changed by (i) hiding the searchword; (ii) suppressing the words/tags/POS tags in the concordance window, and (iii) changing the context type. It is also possible to create a graph of the distribution of hits across the corpus.

8.1 Navigation

Changing from one window to another is accomplished by selecting the desired window from the list in the WINDOW menu. If the CASCADE option in the WINDOW menu is selected, you can simply click on the visible portion of the window you wish to bring to the foreground.

8.2 Change Font and Highlight Font

large fonts

To change the font, font style, font size, or font colour for each language, select CHANGE FONT or CHANGE HIGHLIGHT FONT from the DISPLAY menu.

8.3 Word Wrap

The display of text in the corpus file and in the concordance results (if the context type line or sentence is selected) can be controlled by the WORD WRAP command in the CORPUS TEXT menu and in the DISPLAY menu.

8.4 Suppress Words/Tags

different views

The concordance lines (or corpus) can be "cleaned up" by selecting SUPPRESS from the DISPLAY menu. The choices for suppression are NORMAL TAGS, SPECIAL TAGS and WORDS. Selecting one of these will suppress/display the appearance of the corresponding data structure. Any two of the three data structures can be suppressed at a time.

The form of the tags is specified in TAG SETTINGS in the FILE menu and the program uses this information to hide the tags.

8.5 Distribution

skewed data It is often useful to obtain a sense of the distribution of hits through a corpus. You might want to check for major skewing in the distribution of hits that might be due to an idiosyncratic file or to the different sub-corpora that are present.

Selecting DISTRIBUTION in the DISPLAY menu leads to a graphical display of hits through the corpus or through an individual file.

Warning: If the concordance results window is not active, then the DISTRIBUTION command will not appear.

Also of considerable interest is tracking the distribution of a translation equivalent though the corpus. The diagram below shows the distribution of *head* (in the English corpus) and *tête* (in the French corpus).

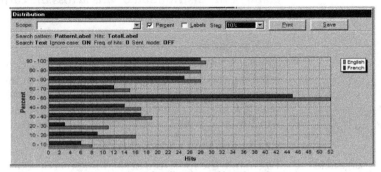

Figure 42: Distribution of head and tête

The x axis indicates the number of hits and the y axis shows the position in the corpus (or in a particular file). If the PERCENT checkbox is deselected, the y axis displays line numbers rather than percentages to indicate position.

The box labelled SCOPE at the top of the screen allows the user to toggle between a display of hits in the entire corpus and the hits in a single file.

In the graph shown, the number of hits are calculated for each 10% of the corpus. Other divisions of the corpus (or file), segments comprising 2%, 5%, 20%, 25%, 33% and 50%, can be set (in STEP at the top of the window).

To print a copy of the table, click on the PRINT button at the top right of the window.

8.6 Locating Hits

tracking info Selecting a line in the concordance results window invokes the display of information about the source of the hit in the lower left of the screen. The information given includes the file name and—if specified in TAG SETTINGS—page number, line number and tracked tags. This information can also be seen by clicking on the line with the right mouse button and choosing DISPLAY INFO.

A window comes into view that provides information on the source file/page/line and on the value of tracked tags. The specification of tags to be tracked is given in TAG SETTINGS (NORMAL TAGS) in the FILE menu.

8.7 Changing the Display: KWIC, Sentence, ...

The form of the context—words, characters, etc.—for the concordance results can be changed via CONTEXT TYPE in the DISPLAY menu. Making the change in SEARCH OPTIONS changes the default; whereas using the command in DISPLAY only alters the form of the current results. After manipulating the data through sorting, deleting etc., it is often beneficial to switch to sentence format in order to import the results into a write-up.

9. Sorting Out Patterns

Summary: The concordance lines can be sorted to reveal patterns in the data. The basic sorting option involves choosing a primary and secondary sort order. More extensive and more complex sorting options are available in ADVANCED SORT.

9.1 Sorting

As mentioned above, the search terms in the concordance window are displayed initially in what is referred to as text order. However, much of the utility of a concordance program derives from its ability to re-sort the items in such a way that similar forms line up together. This re-sorting reveals recurrent patterns in the text, as illustrated earlier with the search for *speak*. Once the concordance lines are sorted in an appropriate manner, the user can scroll though the results to visually identify common patterns.

Aggregating similar patterns is accomplished by ordering the concordance lines so that they are alphabetised according to, for example, the word to the right of the search term. This is a 1ST RIGHT sort. Other similar sorting options are 2ND RIGHT, 1ST LEFT, 2ND LEFT, ORIGINAL TEXT ORDER, or SEARCH TERM. Choosing one of these sort orders specifies the primary sort. Once one item is selected from the SORT menu, the mouse can be moved horizontally to select a second sort, which specifies the secondary sort order. The primary and secondary sort orders 1ST RIGHT, 1ST LEFT and 1ST LEFT, 1ST RIGHT are commonly used and hence are listed separately in the SORT menu.

1st R, 1st L

A 1ST RIGHT, 1ST LEFT sort means that the concordance lines are sorted alphabetically according to the word following the search term, and then, if there are lines in which the same word occurs after the search term, these lines are further sorted according to the alphabetical order of the word preceding the search term.

alphabetical

The particular meaning of alphabetical order is determined by Windows (not by the software) and depends on the language setting in place.

9.2 Advanced Sort

85

An ADVANCED SORT option is divided into two parts. The first, upper component of the dialogue box invoked by the selection of ADVANCED SORT allows the user to choose a primary, secondary and tertiary sort order (labelled as FIRST SORT, SECOND SORT and THIRD SORT).

reverse sort

In addition, for any sort position a reverse sort can be selected. A reverse sort orders the lines in alphabetical order of the endings of words with the result, that *panda,* for instance, comes before *bear.* (This feature may be especially useful if you are working with Arabic or Hebrew.) The second component is a customised sort, which is selected by a checkbox. This provides even more flexibility since the user can enter a range for the sort, such as 3L-3R. This range will sort the lines 3L, 2L, 1L, SW, 1R, 2R and 3R! Alternatively, the user can specify a sequence of sort domains separated by a comma. The terms permitted in this listing are as follows:

3L, 2L, 1L, 1R, 2R, 3R

0 = Seach term

DEF = Defined sort

ORIG = Original order

1Lr = 1st Left, reverse sort

Note: If the customised sort option is checked, it is impossible to select items such as FIRST SORT, SECOND SORT, etc. in the upper portion of the dialogue box.

9.3 User-Defined Sort

grouping

A further option available under ADVANCED SORT is a DEFINED option. This allows the categorisation and grouping (i.e., sorting) of concordance lines according to user-defined categories. Thus if you have five categories or classifications that are appropriate for a set of concordance results, you can assign the letter *a, b, c, d,* or *e,* as appropriate, to each line. To do this, select (click on) a concordance line, click on the right mouse button and assign a letter to that line. (See Figure 12, page 31.) The assigned letter is then displayed to the left of each concordance line. Choosing the DEFINED option in ADVANCED SORT orders the lines according to the letters assigned by the user, which will group the members of each type together.

A further parameter that can be used to sort the concordance lines is Tracked tags.

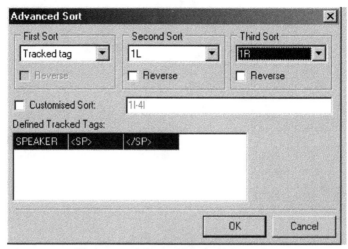

Figure 43: Advanced Sort dialogue box

In the example shown above, the First Sort is defined in terms of the value of the Speaker Tag, which means that the concordance lines will be reordered in a way that clusters the hits associated with each speaker.

In this example, there is only a single tracked tag. If there are multiple Tracked tags, the one to be used in sorting can be selected from the DEFINED TRACKED TAGS box.

10. General Search Control and Search Options

Summary: Settings related to searches are located in SEARCH OPTIONS **and in** GENERAL SEARCH CONTROL **in the** ADVANCED SEARCH **dialogue box.**

customise

The parameters controlling searches are located in two places: GENERAL SEARCH CONTROL in the ADVANCED SEARCH dialogue box and in SEARCH OPTIONS.

The features under GENERAL SEARCH CONTROL (visible in Figure 21 for example) are checkboxes for:

IGNORE CASE OF CHARACTERS

USE SKIPPING AND EQUAL CHARACTERS

SENTENCE MODE

The features under SEARCH OPTIONS are:

MAX SEARCH HITS

FREQUENCY OF HITS

CONTEXT TYPE

Special characters

Range character

TAG SEARCH SEPARATOR

CHARACTERS TO TREAT AS (word) DELIMITERS

SKIPPING CHARACTERS

EQUAL CHARACTERS

Wildcard characters

HEADINGS

10.1 Ignore Case of Letters

The "factory" default is set such that searches that are insensitive to case, that is, a search for **let** will find *Let* and *LET*. To change this setting, simply check (or uncheck) the box labelled IGNORE CASE OF LETTERS in GENERAL SEARCH CONTROL.

case and [a-z]	This setting can have wider ramifications than you might expect. For example, a REGULAR EXPRESSION search for **[A-Z]** will (surprisingly) match a lower case letter if IGNORE CASE OF LETTERS is selected. In addition, the specification in the left and right contexts of context searches is sensitive to this setting, as is the specification of tags in TAG SEARCH.

10.2 Skipping and Equal Characters

skipp=in/g	Selecting the USE SKIPPING AND EQUAL CHARACTERS option by checking the appropriate box in the ADVANCED SEARCH dialogue box brings into force the settings for these two parameters as entered in SEARCH OPTIONS.

The skipping characters are useful for avoiding potential problems with mark-up symbols. It is often the case that words in spoken corpora contain non-alphanumeric symbols that are used to indicate prosodic information. Thus, you may come across different forms of the same word in a spoken corpus: *speaking* and *speak^ing*, for example. This causes a fundamental problem for word searches since a search for **speaking** will miss *speak^ing*. The answer, not surprisingly, is skipping characters. We simply enter ^ in the text box for skipping characters in the SEARCH OPTIONS dialogue box. The result is that a search for **speaking** will find both *speaking* and *speak^ing* (or even *s^p^e^a^k^i^n^g*). Basically, the occurrence of ^ is ignored.

d=t	The EQUAL CHARACTERS option is useful for finding alternative spellings, e.g., making *d* equivalent to *t* (d=t) or for ignoring certain distinctions. Thus if you wanted to disregard the particulars of vowels in a romanised version of Arabic, you could enter a=u=i in the EQUAL CHARACTERS box in SEARCH OPTIONS. If two sets of options are required, they should be separated by a semicolon: d=t; a=u=i.

10.3 Sentence Mode

A search for a phrase, particularly a search using the range wildcard character @, may catch words spread across a sentence boundary with the result that the beginning of the string is in one sentence and the end is in the following sentence. Sometimes this is fine, but nine times out of ten, the user will simply eliminate these examples because they do not fit the desired target pattern. Checking the SENTENCE MODE option in the ADVANCED SEARCH dialogue box restricts the search such that hits are only displayed if all the components of the search string occur within a single sentence.

10.4 Maximum Number of Hits

The maximum number of concordance lines or hits is constrained by various program limitations. The maximum number of concordance lines that can be displayed is no longer limited to 16,000 and so the number of hits can be set to a higher number. However, you may occasionally wish to fix the number of hits. For example, if you are performing several searches, you might want to limit each search to 100 hits, for example.

The factory default setting for the maximum number of hits is 500.

10.5 Frequency of Hits

every nth hit The default value for FREQUENCY OF HITS is 1, which means that every instance of the search term found in the text is displayed in the concordance results window. This is usually what you want, but if you search for a very common word, you may well prefer to gather examples from all the files in your corpus, and not just from the first file that is searched. To allow the sampling of hits from a range of text files, you need to change the value of FREQUENCY OF HITS to a larger number. For instance, entering 5 in FREQUENCY OF HITS in the SEARCH OPTIONS dialog box will result in every 5th hit being displayed.

10.6 Changing Context Type and Size

char/word/line Generally, the context is set so that each context line fills the width of the screen, allowing the results to be viewed easily. This is the traditional KWIC display. However, there are, in total, five context types: characters, words, lines, sentence s and segments. In addition, for all the options apart from sentence, an appropriate size of context can be specified in the relevant units: 40 characters, 8 words, 2 lines etc.

In fact, there are actually two ways in which the context can be set. First of all, the default context type, which controls the way in which the results of each search are initially displayed is set in SEARCH OPTIONS. The same range of settings also appears in CONTEXT TYPE in the DISPLAY menu. Changing the options in the DISPLAY menu only alters the format of the current results window; it does not change the default setting.

Typically, the default context is based on a number of characters or words. This provides a KWIC display, which makes it easy to visually scan the results. The default context for the "non-search" language is segment. Once the appropriate results have been identified, users may want to switch to a sentence context so that the examples can be saved to a file in the form of a series of sentences.

10.7 What is a Word?

It is clear that a prerequisite for a word searching program is a definition of what a word is. This is not a particularly difficult issue in written texts—the first definition of a word that comes to mind is a string of letters (and perhaps numbers) surrounded by spaces. And with a little further thought, we would realise that we need to include punctuation symbols, in addition to spaces, as possible delimiters of words. Hence, we can define a word as a string of characters bounded by either spaces or punctuation (plus special computer characters such as the carriage return).

/.:+word\ #'{-

Let's examine a couple of situations in order to illustrate the subtleties that you are likely to encounter after a little experimentation with concordance searches. To exemplify the complications you might run into, we can consider the first word in the previous sentence. But what is the first word? According to our preliminary definition it is *let*, and the second word is *s*. Similarly, we can ask whether *committee's* should be treated as one word or two. And the same question can be asked concerning *mid-day*, and so on.

ParaConc is initially configured so that by default the apostrophe is taken to be part of a word. This means that a search for *let* will not find *let's* because the latter would count as a 5-character word, whereas the search was for the 3-character word *let*. (To find both *let's* and *let*, we would need to specify the search term **let%%**.) If, on the other hand, the apostrophe counted as a word delimiter, then searching for **let** would find *let's* or at least the first part of *let's*.

The advantage of having the apostrophe be part of a word and not a punctuation character (or word delimiter) is that you can then search for the apostrophe. Thus the search ***'s** would find all possessives, as well as contractions of *is* and *has*. (Note: If you are really interested in possessives in English and want to avoid forms such as *he's* and *it's*, you can ensure that the string before the possessive is at least three characters long by using the search query **???*'s**.)

If you decide that you want to change the search parameters so that *let's* and *let* would both be found by a search for **let**, then you simply select SEARCH OPTIONS and add the apostrophe to the characters that define a word boundary. These characters, the word delimiters, are listed in a text box, and characters can be added or removed from the list by simply typing in or deleting the appropriate characters. In this case, we need to click in the text box and type in the apostrophe character.

error message

Having made this change, we can now search for **let** and find *let's*. On the other hand, a search for **???*'s** will now cause an error message to be displayed, because it is not possible include a delimiter character in a search. (Space is

92

an exception to this rule. It is, of course, possible to include a space in the search string and space will then match any delimiter.)

Let's run through a couple more examples. If you wish to search for sentence boundaries, you can remove "." from the list of delimiters and search for *. .(Don't make the mistake of searching for . alone. This would only work if there were a space between the last word in the sentence and the full stop.) Along similar lines, you might be interested in examining sentence-initial occurrences of a word such as *first*. In this case, you can search for *. First (assuming that there are no tags indicating a sentence boundary). And, a sentence-initial active participle may be captured with *. *ing.

factory setting Clicking on the drop down arrow at the end of the delimiter box will reveal a list of previous settings for word delimiters. Any of these previous settings can be restored if necessary. It is also possible to restore the original "factory" setting for the list of word delimiters by selecting the button REVERT TO DEFAULT in the SEARCH OPTIONS dialogue box.

10.8 Changing the Wildcard Characters

search for % In discussing search options above, we saw the usefulness of % as a wildcard character. But what if we want to search for % as a literal in *100%*? To allow a search for %, it is necessary to first replace % as a wildcard symbol, perhaps with $, so that %, as %, can be searched for. To do this, select SEARCH OPTIONS and simply substitute $ in the 'zero or one character box' in the SEARCH OPTIONS dialogue box. We can then search for % with the character then being treated literally as a percent sign rather than as a wildcard character.

The other wildcard characters ? (exactly 1 character) and * (0 or more characters) and the range character @ can be replaced in the same way. It is also possible to change the word-tag delimiter (&) used in tag searches.

10.9 Headings

Before a heading search can be performed, it is necessary to specify the tags that define the heading and the body. The dialogue box to do this can be accessed from SEARCH OPTIONS or via EDIT in the HEADINGS/CONTEXTS SEARCH dialogue box.

11. Working with languages other than English

11.1 File Format

The appropriate format for *ParaConc* files is ANSI (Windows text). If your non-English files are in ASCII format and you load them into *ParaConc*, then the accents will appear garbled. You need to load the files into a Windows word processor such as Word, making use of the appropriate code page, and then save the files (with a different name) as text files.

ParaConc cannot work directly with Unicode files, but it does convert Unicode into ANSI. After loading Unicode files, select them all and then check the UTF-8 box.

11.2 Entering Accented Characters

Choosing the appropriate language before loading a corpus helps to make the software work appropriately. Choosing a language will not change the keyboard, however, making it difficult to enter special characters such as ç and é to give examples from French. In order to make it easy to enter these characters in the search string, a French virtual keyboard must be installed. To do this, select Control Panel under Settings in the Windows Start menu. Click on Keyboard and follow the directions for installing keyboards for different languages. Once installed, you can use the ALT to switch from one keyboard to the next.

Many of the language-related settings of ParaConc come from Windows, which means that the easiest way to work with Chinese, for example, is to install the program on a computer running the Chinese Windows operating system.

11.3 Collocate Span

A span of 2L-2R works quite well for English, but the default span for other languages such as French might be better set at 3L-3R. For information on finding collocates in CJK, see the following section.

11.4 Working with Chinese, Japanese, Korean

Chinese, Japanese, Korean, and other two-byte languages which do not use spaces to indicate word boundaries present particular problems for a concordancer, which is a word-based searching program. It is, nevertheless, possible to use *ParaConc* to search CJK texts, sort the results, and obtain some basic colllocational information.

It is important to choose the appropriate language/encoding system before loading the files.

In most representations, CJK are displayed without spaces between words and a special segmentation program is needed to add spaces or other indicators of a word boundary in the appropriate places—a process that is not trivial. If the text has been segmented, then the ordinary text search will work, as long as the word boundary indicator is listed in the Word Delimiter textbox.

If the text is not segmented, then the simple text search option cannot be used and searching must be done using the regex search option, which is a part of the ADVANCED SEARCH command. This allows all the instances of the search string in a text to be displayed in a KWIC format, in the usual way.

That is the good news. The bad news is that the absence of word boundaries means that it is impossible to look at the collocates of the search string. The only manipulation of the search results that is possible is a right sort. A left sort will be meaningless in this situation since what is interpreted as a word boundary could be anywhere in the preceding string, although one option is to use the reverse option for a Left Sort in the Advanced Sort command. This will sort the characters based on the character immediately preceding the search string.

Left and Right Sort

The easiest manipulation of the search results a 1st Right, 2nd Right sort. A regular left sort will be meaningless in this situation since what is interpreted as a word boundary could be anywhere in the preceding string which means that the characters appearing immediately before the search term would not show any patterning. However, if a left sort is required, we can use ADVANCED SORT, selecting Left Sort and checking the box for the Reverse option. This option ensures that the ordering is based on the character at the end of the "word" rather than the beginning, thus sorting the results based on the character immediately preceding the search string.

Collocates

Since there are no word boundaries, the collocate frequency cannot be used, but it is possible to obtain some collocate information by the following technique. If we wish to get a sense of the collocates following XXX, then in the regex search box we enter XXX followed by two dots (..) for each character, thus the most likely options are XXX.. and XXX.... (and of course the wild card characters can precede XXX if necessary). Next we choose ADVANCED COLLOCATION, selecting SEARCH TERM for the first position and none for the other positions. The result will be a frequency list.

12. Parallel Corpora and Language Learning

Barlow (1996) suggested that parallel texts provide a useful resource for language learning by allowing learners to examine the correspondences between words and structures in two languages. Any exploitation of parallel corpora is likely to follow the general data-driven learning approach in which students are led through the manipulation of corpus data or through the questions posed to them to a raised awareness of target structures, particularly those that differ from L1 in a way that causes difficulties for learners.

Initially, the use of parallel texts may simply be highlighting the lack of a one-to-one correspondence between words in L1 and L2 and one aspect of such exercises might usefully involve an examination of false friends. Tasks that involve the exploration and analysis of a distinction made in L2, but not in L1 are potentially more difficult, but nonetheless potentially very useful for the student.

The analysis of learner corpora has revealed the tendency of L2 writers to overuse certain words or constructions, whether adverbs or connectors or extraposed *it* sentences. This may be due to learner input from textbooks or a consequence of the influence of L1. More advanced students can use parallel texts to build up their knowledge of new meanings of known words, collocational structures or, more generally, preferred ways of saying things in L2.

Language learners often face some difficulty interpreting concordance lines in the target language, hindering their ability to observe and absorb new language patterns. One use of parallel texts is to provide L1 support for the student's investigations of L2 as noted by Chujo et al. (2008) in a paper describing the use concordance-based DDL exercises for Japanese learners of English.

> With the development of parallel corpus concordancing programs, the Japanese translation allows learners to understand the target language

concordance lines and provides a
richer context in both languages,
enabling an inductive approach to
understanding patterning in both
languages in authentic data and to
forming generalizations about
language form and use.

This may work particularly well in Japan where students
are very used to accessing electronic dictionaries, making
translation support for concordance lines a natural
extension of common student behaviour and it turns out
that Chujo et al report generally positive outcomes in terms
of learning and attitudes.

12.1 Syllabus design

The design of a language syllabus involves many factors,
including the aims of the learners for whom the course is
designed, but one important factor is an accurate
description of the target language, whether it is American
English used in business settings or technical articles
written in German. There is an increasing use of corpora to
determine the optimal content of language courses and as
part of what is known as data-driven learning (DDL). DDL
is the term used by Johns (1994) for language learning
activities in which corpus data is analysed by students as
part of a discovery learning approach to grammar. Students
are asked to identify and classify language patterns, thus
raising awareness of the target language and doing so in a
way that helps to entrench the target patterns.

In practice, a description of the language has typically not
been based on actual usage, but on a mixture of tradition
and intuition (Tomlinson 1998:87).

The language syllabus has often been structured around the
presentation of different grammatical tenses, with the
dough of grammatical structures leavened with some
language functions such as introductions, apologies, and so
on. In the majority of cases, however, neither the structural
nor the functional components have been derived from an
empirical investigation due to both the approach taken to
theoretical linguistics and the tradition of language
pedagogy, which has not emphasised language description.

The move from some imagined, idealised notions of the
target language to usage-based descriptions raises a host of
difficult questions due to the very fact that appropriate
target behaviour must be identified. The addition of a

contrastive, parallel component may be beneficial under certain circumstances.

13. Tricks and Tips: Some Final Comments

As you get used to the different options and settings in *ParaConc*, you will become more skilled in exploiting different working techniques to manipulate your results in the way that gets as close as possible to the desired goal. In this final section, we provide a miscellany of techniques for working with *MP* 2.2.

13.1 Counting the search term

If you perform a search containing some kind of wild card character, then you are like to retrieve different keywords or phrases. Thus a search for *self will find *self* plus *myself, yourself*, etc. How do we then get the program to count the individual instances of the words found? The answer is to use the ADVANCED COLLOCATION command. Choose this command and then set the First Sort to Search Item and the Second and Third Sort Items to None. Click on OK and the count of the different forms of *self* will appear in a results textbox.

13.2 Finding hapax legomena

To find all the words that occur only once in a corpus, you simply set both the MINIMUM FREQUENCY and the MAXIMUM FREQUENCY to 1 in FREQUENCY OPTIONS and create a frequency list, which will be displayed in alphabetical order. As always, you should check the word delimiters and the case-sensitive settings to make sure that the results are as required.

13.3 Improving Precision of Searches

Probably the best way to improve the accuracy of searches is to take the time to master regex searches. Simply using the OR option and the optional character ? will make searches easier and more accurate. And with some practice it should be possible to create quite complex search patterns.

In general, then, we can improve precision in a number of ways:

> use regex
>
> lengthen search term

use sentence mode where appropriate

make searches case-sensitive

13.4 Extracting Collocations

Collocations are tied to search terms and so there is no way to simply extract the collocations in a text. However, if you enter a group of words, such as an academic word list and have the program search for all the terms, you can then use the SPAN option in ADVANCED COLLOCATION to present all the two word (or three word, etc.) collocations in frequency order.

REFERENCES

Aijmer, K. and B.Altenberg (eds.) 1991. *English Corpus Linguistics: Studies in Honour of Jan Svartik.* London: Longman.

Aijmer, K., B. Altenberg and M. Johansson. 1996 "Text-based contrastive studies in English. Presentation of a project." In Aijmer, K., Altenberg, B. and Johansson, M. (eds) *Languages in Contrast: Papers from a Symposium on Text-based Cross-linguistic Studies,* Lund 4-5 March 1994. Lund: Lund University Press. 73-85.

Baker 1996. Corpus-based Translation Studies: The Challenges that Lie Ahead', in Harold Somers (ed) *Terminology, LSP and Translation: Studies in Language Engineering in Honour of Juan C. Sager,* Amsterdam & Philadelphia: John Benjamins.

Barlow, M. 1996. Parallel Texts in Language Teaching. In Botley et al. (eds.) *Proceedings of Teaching and Language Corpora.* 45-56

Biber, D. 1988. *Variation across speech and writing.* Cambridge: Cambridge University Press.

Biber, D. 1993. Representativeness in corpus design. *Literary and Linguistic Computing,* 8, 4, 243-257.

Carroll, J.B., P. Davis and B.Richman 1971. *The American Heritage word frequency book.* New York: Houghton Mifflin.

Chafe, Wallace, John W. Du Bois and Sandra A. Thompson. 1991. Towards a new corpus of Spoken American English. In Aijmer, Karin and Bengt Altenberg (eds.) 64-82.

Chujo, K, K. Oghigian and C. Nishigaki. 2008. Hands-on Japanese-English Parallel Corpus Experience in the EFL CALL Classroom. 25th International Conference of English Teaching and Learning 2008 International Conference on English Instruction and Assessment

Francis, W. N. and H. Kucera. 1964. *Manual of information to accompany 'A standard sample of present-day edited American English for use with digital computers'* (revised 1979) Providence, Rhode Island: Department of Linguistics, Brown University

Gale, W. A. and K. W. Church. 1993 "A program for aligning sentences in bilingual corpora." *Computational Linguistics,* 19, 75-102.

Gellerstam, Martin. 1996 "Translations as a source for cross-linguistic studies". In Aijmer, K., Altenberg, B. and Johansson, M. (eds) *Languages in Contrast: Papers from a Symposium on Text-based Cross-linguistic Studies*, Lund 4-5 March 1994. Lund: Lund University Press. 53-62.

Hunston, S. and Sinclair, J. 2000. A Local Grammar of Evaluation in S. Hunston S. and G. Thompson (eds), *Evaluation in Text: Authorial Stance and the Construction of Discourse*. Oxford: Oxford University Press.

Johns, T. 1994. From printout to handout: Grammar and vocabulary teaching in the context of Data-driven Learning." In T. Odlin, ed., *Perspectives on Pedagogical Grammar*. New York: Cambridge University Press.

Kelljmer, G. 1994. *A Dictionary of English Collocations Based on the Brown Corpus* Oxford Clarendon Press.

Kemmer, S. and M. Barlow. Introduction: A Usage-Based Conception of Language. In M. Barlow and S. Kemmer (eds), *Usage-Based Models of Language*. 7-28, 2000.

Kenny, D. 1999. Norms and creativity: Lexis in translated text. PhD Thesis. UMIST.

Kufner, H.L. 1962. *The Grammatical Structures of English and German*. Chicago.

Langacker, R. 1987. *Foundations of Cognitive Grammar Vol. 1: Theoretical Prerequisites*. Stanford: Stanford University Press.

Langacker, R. 1988. A usage-based model. In B. Rudzka-Ostyn, (ed), *Topics in Cognitive Linguistics*, 127-61. Amsterdam: Benjamins.

Langacker, R. 2000. A dynamic usage-based model. . In M. Barlow and S. Kemmer (eds), *Usage- Based Models of Language*. 1-63, Stanford: CSLI.

Laufer, B. 1994. The lexical profile of second language writing: Does it change over time? *RELC Journal* 25: 21-33.

Laviosa, S. 2002. *Corpus-based Translation Studies. Theory, Findings, Applications*. Amsterdam and New York: Rodopi.

McCarthy, M. 2002. What is an advanced level vocabulary. In M. Tan (ed.) *Corpus studies in language education*. Bangkok: IELE Press. 15-29

Moropa, K. 2007. Analysing the English-Xhosa Parallel Corpus of Technical Texts with Paraconc: A Case Study of Term Formation Processes. *Southern African Linguistics and Applied Language Studies*, 2007, 25, 2, 183-205

Moulton, W. G. 1962. *The Sounds of English and German.* Chicago.

Nickel, Gerhard. 1971. "Contrastive Linguistics and foreign-language teaching." In G. Nickel (ed). *Papers in Contrastive Linguistics.* Cambridge: CUP.1-16.

Ooi,Vincent B, Y. 1998. *Computer Corpus Lexicography.* Edinburgh Textbooks in Empirical Linguistics. Edinburgh: Edinburgh University Press.

Pawley, A. and F. Syder. 1983 Two puzzles for linguistic theory: nativelike selection and nativelike fluency. In J. C. Richards and R. W. Schmidt, RW, *Language and Communication,* Longman.

Sinclair, John. 1991. *Corpus, Concordance, Collocation.* Oxford: Oxford University Press.

Tan, Melinda. (ed.) 2002. *Corpus studies in language education.* Bangkok: IELE Press.

Tognini-Bonelli, E. 2001. *Corpus Linguistics at Work.* Amsterdam: John Benjamins

Tomlinson, B, 1998. *Materials Development in Language Teaching.* Cambridge: Cambridge University Press.

Toury, G. 1986. Monitoring discourse transfer: A test case for a developmental model of translation. In J. House and S. Blum-Kulka (eds) *Interlingual and Intercultural Communication: Discourse and Cognition in Translation and Second Language Acquisition Studies* 79-94. Tübingen: Narr

Váradi T. and Kiss, G. 2001. Equivalence and Non-equivalence in Parallel Corpora . *International Corpus of Corpus Linguistics.* 6, 167-177

Wu, Y-P and Chang, Y-C. 2008. Chinese Translation of Literary Black Dialect and Translation Strategy Reconsidered: The Case of Alice Walker's *The Color Purple. Literary Translations* 12, 1

http://www.accurapid.com/journal/43colorpurple.htm

INDEX

www.ingramcontent.com/pod-product-compliance
Lightning Source LLC
Chambersburg PA
CBHW071229050326
40689CB00011B/2498